# Unless Recalled Earlier

## DATE DUE

# AFFLUENT REVOLUTIONARIES

# AFFLUENT REVOLUTIONARIES
## A PORTRAIT OF THE NEW LEFT

STEPHEN GOODE

New Viewpoints
*A Division of Franklin Watts, Inc.*
New York | 1974

*For my mother and father*

First NEW VIEWPOINTS edition, 1974
Copyright © 1974 by Stephen Goode
Originally published by Franklin Watts, Inc. 1974

**Library of Congress Cataloging in Publication Data**

Goode, Stephen,
  Affluent revolutionaries.
  (Studies in contemporary politics)
  Bibliography: p.
  1. Radicalism.  2. Revolutionists.  3. Right and
left (Political science)  I. Title.
HN18.G59     322.4'2     73-8953
ISBN 0-531-02645-0
ISBN 0-531-05557-4 (pbk.)

# CONTENTS

# INTRODUCTION

The new radicalism of the 1960s discussed in this book was both a revival of leftist politics and a revolt of the young against an older generation. The two have not always gone hand in hand. Older people have often been the most successful revolutionaries, and the young have frequently chosen means other than politics to reject their parents and discover new ways of living.

Leftist politics are as old as the French Revolution. The designation "left" was given to those who sat on the left side of the revolutionary assembly in Paris and who tended to be more radical than the delegates who sat on the right. To be left has meant that one prefers change and reform to happen more rapidly. It has also meant that one advocates more equal distribution of wealth and property and less poverty and want. Some leftists have been moderates and have believed that change could come gradually. Others have been more radical and have demanded total destruction of the old ways of life and construction of new systems of government.

Youthful rebellion has manifested itself in a thousand ways. Among some young people toward the beginning of the nineteenth century, it caused a movement called Romanticism. The young revived old customs, and fell in love with the mystery of the past. They fell deeply and passionately in love with one another and sometimes committed suicide when unhappiness inevitably came. The idea of the Romantics was to live life to its fullest and not submit to the dictates of reason and order.

In the twentieth century, in the decade of the sixties alone, the energy of the young found numerous expressions. Some became hippies and returned to nature, turning their backs on modern society and its noise and pollution. Others took up spiritual interests and found meaning in yoga and the religions of the East. Some found that the beliefs of fundamentalist Christianity answered the difficult questions of life. Others took part in all of these movements.

Finally, a large number of young people expressed their rebellion by turning to politics and taking up the causes of the left. Their energy and vitality were put into reforms and the establishment of a more equal, just society. These were the young men and women who formed the radical movement we call the New Left. They found in revolution and social radicalism the meaning that others of their generation found in "dropping out" or in religion. They developed an almost mystic belief in the power of political action as they attacked glaring problems of inequality, war, and big government. They were full of idealism and hope that the future would be better than the past; they felt assured that they could make a better world than their parents had.

This, then, is the story of the young political activists of the 1960s. The first part of the book tells of the New Left in 1968, at the height of its activity, and describes the movement's heroes, art, film, and thought. The next section traces the origin and history of the new radicalism in America, western Europe, and Japan. The final two chapters discuss other youth movements of the past and set forth conclusions about youthful politics and the New Left. This introduction to the movement, it is believed, justly credits its hopes and idealism, while noting well its mistakes and extremes.

# 1 THE WATERSHED YEAR

Nineteen sixty-eight was the year of the New Left. Students throughout the world captured universities, marched in demonstrations, and fought police. Thousands of young people called themselves revolutionaries and spoke of overthrowing the system. Rarely a day passed when the newspapers or television did not carry some news of fresh student demands; magazines were filled with pictures of young men and women waving the red flags of radical socialism or the black flags of anarchism.

This radical activity struck most deeply into the advanced, industrialized democracies of western Europe, Japan, and the United States. Students had been rebelling for years in Latin America and in other underdeveloped areas where poverty and hunger existed, but no one expected that the young people of the wealthy, privileged nations would turn against their parents and their governments with so much anger and resentment.

Revolutions have often come with spring, after the cold days have gone. The student in-

1

surrections of 1968 followed this time-honored tradition. In Paris and New York, many a young man's fancy turned to barricades and revolt rather than to thoughts of love. At Columbia University in New York events leading to the seizure of the university began in March; in France, a radical student committee was formed at Nanterre University on March 22. What sprouted in early spring would come to full blossom by summer of that year.

Student radicalism at Columbia University centered around two problems. First, the students opposed expansion of the university into Harlem, the predominantly black area adjacent to the campus. They argued that Columbia gave no consideration to black people. The university wanted to build a gymnasium on land that had been a park and, according to the students, had not asked the people of the neighborhood if they resented the loss of the park. Student radicals took up the cause in order to save the land and give the blacks a voice in how their community was run.

The second issue that inspired the radicals at Columbia in the spring of 1968 was the university's connection with the Institute for Defense Analysis, called IDA. IDA was a government-financed institution that dealt with the problems of waging war. It hired professors to do research and used university property to develop and test weapons being used in Vietnam. The young radicals thought that the university should have nothing to do with the war, which they deeply opposed.

However, the opposition to both the gymnasium and to IDA reflected a still deeper concern among the students. What they really found unacceptable and struggled against was the largeness and remoteness of many American institutions, from Columbia University to the federal government itself. They felt that power had been taken from the common man and had been given to a few privileged bureaucrats who ran the universities and government agencies. American society was tyrannical and authoritarian and had forgotten its democratic tradition of fair play and participation by all citizens.

Radical students planned to use Columbia as a test case. Months earlier, they had decided to confront the power structure of the university and expose its corruption and authoritarianism. Columbia University was to be used as a means of "enlightening" the American public and showing the people that revolution was needed. The student radicals thought they could start a mass movement for reform and change.

Student discontent had become obvious by March, but it was not until April 23 that the insurrection actually began. Large groups of students protested, chanting "IDA must go, IDA must go," and "racist gym must go, racist gym must go." Mark Rudd, head of Columbia's Students for a Democratic Society (SDS), and a spokesman for the white radicals on campus, made speeches denouncing university power, racism, and American imperialism. Some of his followers tore down part of the fence surrounding the gymnasium construction site. The radicals presented the university with a list of demands which asked that IDA be removed, that the construction of the gymnasium be stopped, and that no student who took part in the insurrection be penalized in any way.

The students occupied Hamilton Hall, an administration and classroom building, and held a dean prisoner in his own office. Throughout the night the students debated what to do and how far to carry their revolution. In the morning, the black radicals asked the whites to leave. Black students had separate grievances from whites and wanted to establish their own movement and create their own voice of protest. While rejecting white middle-class values, many black students desired for their own people the affluence and power found in the homes the white radicals had left and rejected.

The whites reluctantly agreed to leave and walked across the campus to another building, Low Library, where the offices of the president and vice-president were located. This building, too, was seized, as well as another classroom building, and the white students broke into the president's office, drank his sherry, and smoked his cigars. There was an air of celebration about the occupation of the president's well-furnished office—the young revolutionaries had at last come to a center of what they considered ultimate power.

For the next several days the university simmered. Conservative and moderate students resented deeply the disruption of classes and university activity. Some athletes attempted to attack the radicals, but were held back by the campus police. The nonradical students milled about and hoped that something would be done to open the school.

The faculty and administration, under President Grayson Kirk, seemed incapable of deciding what should be done. The university had been taken aback by the guerrilla tactics of the students and no plan of action had been developed to handle student insurrection. The radicals themselves confused the faculty and administration even further by rejecting compromise and by changing their demands from time to time. The student plan was to disrupt the school totally and bring Columbia to its knees.

The students held the occupied buildings for seven days, then the president of the university, over the protest of the faculty, asked the city police to come onto university property to restore order. Blacks, many of whom had knowledge of police techniques, left Columbia without a fight. Many white students and young faculty members remained to be arrested. Some were reported to have been beaten, clubbed, and dragged to the waiting police vans. Altogether, some six hundred young people were detained.

When the smoke cleared and calm returned to Columbia, the radicals found that they had achieved many of their goals. President Kirk resigned and both IDA and the gymnasium were under severe attack from the faculty. A report by a special committee of unbiased observers, chaired by Archibald Cox, dean of the Harvard Law School, found many student grievances to be valid. According to the committee, the university was too big and too insensitive to students and to those who lived in the neighborhood of the campus.

But the majority of Americans were critical of the Columbia students and felt no sympathy for student causes. People across the country asked why the privileged few should be permitted to demonstrate and rebel, while other young people were dying in Vietnam or working regular shifts at factories and businesses. The students had hoped to arouse sympathy among "the people" in their fight against oppression, but instead they aroused only ill will and resentment.

Radicals, in this instance, had achieved some of their short-term goals, but had failed in the long-term goal of stirring up revolutionary sentiment throughout the country.

The New Left produced further ill will and resentment a few months later at the convention of the Democratic party in Chicago. The Columbia insurrection had been the first major revolutionary incident of 1968; the convention was to be the second. Thousands of young radicals of many different political beliefs poured into Chicago in August to confront the party held most responsible for the Vietnam War. Among the young people there were moderate leftists who supported Senator Eugene McCarthy, one of the candidates for the presidential nomination. The McCarthy supporters had come to participate in the "democratic process" and to demonstrate for their cause in an orderly and responsible manner. A more radical group who called themselves "yippies" had come to mock the convention by nominating their own candidate, a pig they called Pigasus. Still others had come simply to confront and harass delegates and the police.

The result was a disaster. Policemen overreacted to the disruption and clubbed radicals mercilessly. The convention itself was a near shambles as delegates came to blows over whether they should support the demonstrators and young radicals or the police. Millions of the Americans who watched the convention on television felt the radicals had presented them with a spectacle they wanted to forget. The majority of the country condemned the young and praised the police.

Nineteen sixty-eight was indeed the year of the New Left in America, but it had become impossible to understand what the radicals were doing. They had made themselves seen, to be sure. But they had also made themselves hated and feared. The mass support they hoped for was never achieved; and they had succeeded in isolating themselves from the influence and power they sought.

. . .

The issues of the French student revolt of 1968 were similar to the issues argued by the Columbia University radicals. The French students felt threatened by the size of their universities and accused them of being insensitive to students and their needs. They also accused the universities of close collaboration with middle-class society and with what they considered the repressive government of Charles de Gaulle. For young French radicals, as for their American counterparts, the university had become an arm of the tyrannical, unjust establishment that they condemned so roundly.

French student activity came to a head in April and early May. In Nanterre, a suburb west of Paris, the rector of the university, where student protest had been spreading since March 22, closed down the institution. He feared a clash between the right-wing students and radicals. Left-wing students marched into Paris, where they were joined by many young students of the Sorbonne, the University of Paris. The students reacted as the young French revolutionaries of 1789, 1848–1849, and 1871 had reacted: they tore up the pavement; upset vehicles, in this case an estimated 188 cars; and made barricades to defend themselves against the police. Violent clashes followed and many young people as well as policemen were injured. French police and helmeted students fought viciously with rocks, clubs, and fists.

For thirty-four days the students occupied the Sorbonne. The Latin Quarter of Paris, the area around the university, was closed off; the students directed traffic and the police did not enter the area. All across France university students rebelled, trying to imitate the radicals of the capital. But the most significant event of the revolution was the momentary unity of the French worker with the student. In America, the workers had taken an overwhelmingly antistudent stand and had frequently attacked young demonstrators. In France, at least for a few days, workers and students both struck against the government of Charles de Gaulle, demanding changes.

Nearly a million workers and students marched together in Paris on May 13. But the union of student and worker, as the union of white and black radicals at Columbia, was short-lived. The interests and demands of French student and worker diverged radically. Workers wanted better hours and higher wages; students wanted more ambiguous changes such as less bureaucracy and less emphasis on material values and possessions. At one point during May, radicals had attacked and damaged the stock exchange of Paris, demanding an end to capitalism, poverty, and economic exploitation. The attitudes of the students and workers toward automobiles reveals a great deal about their differences. The students' destruction of automobiles was shocking to the French working class. To the French worker an automobile was a symbol of freedom: something to work for and take pride in; to the student, it was the symbol of all that was wrong with capitalism and modern society.

De Gaulle used the differences of interest to divide his opposition. To the workers and unions he granted higher wages and better working conditions. At the same time, steps were taken to outlaw radical student organizations and bring an end to the activism of the universities. Satisfied with their gains, the workers did not protest the problems of the students. When elections were held in June, there was a Gaullist landslide. The students, who had shouted "de Gaulle, adieu," during the height of their demonstrations, found the general more firmly entrenched than ever. The New Left in France had become as well known and as alone as the New Left of the United States.

The major radical movements of 1968 had taken place in France and the United States. But other developed countries had their New Left crusades too. Germany had seen violent demonstrations in 1967, which increased in intensity early in 1968 with the attempted assassination by a right-wing house painter of Rudi Dutschke, a young radical leader. Japanese students protested the Vietnamese War and tried to halt the transportation of American war supplies to Southeast Asia. In Great Britain and Italy universities were threatened and occupied. Everywhere the cry was against American aggression and expansion, against bigness and bureaucracy, against more and more material possessions without improvement of man's social and spiritual situation. Young people found the world their parents had made to be unhealthy, miserable, and rotten. They wanted to change it.

The dramatic events of 1968 had shaken institutions and traditions in western Europe and America. Revolutionaries had failed to make a "revolution," but they had brought to the attention of the public new problems and possible solutions. The year 1968 had not been a "turning point" in history, but it had seen the flowering of a new leftist movement. For many people, the failure of the New Left to take power and change society was not important. It was significant that a new political and social consciousness had developed among the young, a new way of looking at things that would perhaps bear fruit in later years. It is now time to look more closely at the thought and ideas of the new radicalism and to examine its heroes, its art, and its film.

# 2 THE HEROES, IDOLS, ART, AND THOUGHT OF THE NEW LEFT

A political movement is defined by the hopes of its members and its choice of idols. What the group holds sacred, what it chooses to admire and imitate, and what words it uses to describe its desires are important to examine for they complete the picture given by its activity and accomplishments. The New Left was a highly visible movement not only because of its violence and anarchy, but also because its art, its heroes, and its thought were widely displayed and discussed on television and in magazines, newspapers, and books. Perhaps no youth movement of the past has had its goals and purposes so prominently brought before the general public. The media thrived on the flamboyance and daring of the young radicals, and the radicals enjoyed the fame and coverage their thought and actions brought.

Most visible to the general public were the idols and heroes whom thousands of young people chose to imitate. Their faces appeared everywhere—on posters on the walls of dormitories and coffee houses, on magazine covers, and on television. Their books became best sellers and their styles of clothing were copied all over the world. Universities and colleges established new courses to deal with them and to win back the interest of radical students.

These idols and heroes can be divided into two groups. First, and most important, were the revolutionaries—men who were central actors in successful revolutions of the past, or who were waging revolution in our own time against what were considered to be the repressive governments and imperialism of the United States and the Western World. Next, and less significant, were figures from "underground culture" and literature, who caught the imagination of the New Left because they dared to live and think outside of accepted society. These men were not so much political as poetic, eccentric, or dramatically antisocial.

First and foremost among the revolutionary idols of the New Left was Che Guevara. Guevara was a romantic, legendary figure. He had rejected his middle-class Argentinean background and medical education to join Fidel Castro in Cuba and to help lead the revolution against the dictatorship of Fulgencio Battista. When the Cuban Revolution was successfully established, he left the ease and security of Havana to return to Latin America and join revolutionaries in Bolivia.

Che never gave up his devotion to revolution; he continued to fight on the side of the oppressed and exploited. He maintained his optimism about the success of all revolution and spoke in glowing terms of the just society that would come once this present era of warfare was over. When he was killed in Bolivia by government troops, which some people said were trained by the CIA, many of the New Left wept openly and vowed to carry on Che's struggle.

Che's appeal came from his dedication to revolution and his success as a revolutionary. Young radicals could find new meaning for life through Che's example and saw in him a man who was victorious in his fight against society. Che's books and diaries sold well in America and Europe. Speeches of New Left leaders were laced with quotes of his words and references to his activities. Thousands of young men and women copied his clothing and wore the army fatigues and beret made famous by a poster of him that sold around the world. Critics of the New Left said that the young radicals who stormed Berkeley, Columbia, Berlin, or the Sorbonne often looked like large groups of Che Guevara dolls unleashed against the centers of capitalist power.

Mao Tse-tung and, to a lesser degree, Ho Chi Minh, were likewise idolized. Mao had been the leader of the most dramatic and largest revolution of all time—the communist revolution in China, and Ho was head of a small, relatively weak country at war with the United States. Both had been lifelong revolutionaries and were now old men, but they were exempt from the blanket condemnation of those over thirty. To the young revolutionaries, Mao and Ho were examples of men who had not sold out or become corrupt. For them, Mao and Ho had preserved their original revolutionary honesty and vigor. It is important to realize that both Mao and Ho offered many young radicals new, alternative meanings for life and were not merely names dragged up to challenge their parents and those in power. As with Che, many students copied Mao's clothing, and some imitated his simple, austere life. Mao's *Little Red Book* of quotations and thoughts became a best seller. Posters of Mao and Ho were as widespread as those of Che, and the radicals paid further tribute to Ho Chi Minh by using his name as a chant during antiwar demonstrations.

Lesser idols and heroes were taken from other revolutionary movements of the Third World. Many of the New Left supported Al Fatah, the group of Arab revolutionaries that resorted to airplane highjacking and other acts of terrorism in its continuing war with Israel. For the New Left, Israel became a symbol of American power and aggression, and the Arabs were another people victimized by imperialism and exploitation. Revolutionary movements of Africa and South America were spoken of with deep reverence and devotion. Many young radicals dreamed of working with Boumedienne in the building of an independent and revolutionary Algeria, or of fighting with the Tupamaros guerrillas of Uruguay in their struggle for economic and social democracy.

Revolutionary heroes and idols were also taken from the

past. Marx, Lenin, Trotsky, and other individuals connected with the Russian Revolution and communism were admired and talked about. Posters of Marx and Lenin were popular, and some students read deeply in their writings. It was not the communist ideas that made their writings popular, but their connections with a revolutionary past. It is significant that no New Left idol or hero was chosen from the French or American Revolution; French and American revolutionaries had lost their power to stir blood and anger—they were now part of history and were considered bourgeois. Marx or Lenin, however, could raise tempers and fear among the older generation and those in power. This was especially true in America, where leftist causes and radicalism had a short history and where anticommunism was still a strong and influential movement.

Revolutionary idols were also taken from among the black radicals of the United States. Eldridge Cleaver, Hughie Newton, Angela Davis, and others were read and talked about throughout the world. The Black Panther Party was admired as one of the most dedicated and advanced revolutionary groups to be found anywhere and radicals of Paris and Berlin sought to imitate its vigor and commitment.

Black revolutionary leaders drew large audiences when they spoke of the need for lasting, violent change and demanded an end to racism and exploitation. Black rhetoric was often deeply violent and emotional. It called for the murder of whites and the destruction of white property. It issued an ultimatum to white America requiring that millions of dollars be given to blacks in reparation for centuries of slavery and brutality. The rhetoric was for the most part a way to vent anger and resentment, but, at times, the spectacle of groups of white radicals listening and nodding agreement with the black radicals as they asked for white blood was ironic and frightening.

Posters were made of the leading black revolutionaries. The works of black writers joined those of Mao and Che on the shelves of radical bookstores. The most popular of the books by black authors were Eldridge Cleaver's *Soul on Ice* and George Jackson's *Soledad Brother.*

Cleaver was one of the leading Panthers and had been in

and out of prison on a variety of charges. After writing *Soul on Ice,* he left the United States and what he felt to be his political persecution there. For a while he lived with a community of American Black Panther exiles in Algiers, but even socialist Algeria found the Panthers unacceptable, and at this time Cleaver is a man without a country. He has sought asylum in France, only to meet with rejection; perhaps eventually he will be forced to return to the United States.

*Soul on Ice* is a devastating attack upon American society and upon white people. In it, Cleaver documented the racism that he felt had warped his own life and ruined the lives of many black people. He condemned the white man who lied, murdered, and cheated in order to preserve his power and top place in society. Cleaver argued that the white man did not see things the way they really were because he was blinded by belief in his own superiority. He went further and said the white race was death-oriented and had brought destruction and violence upon the rest of the world and upon the colored peoples of America. Cleaver's book was an angry one and was written with the blood and sweat of a man who was tired of seeing his people exploited.

*Soul on Ice* was popular with the New Left because it bitterly attacked America; but the book also held other interests for white radicals. *Soul on Ice* boiled over with life and experience. Cleaver had seen more and done more in his lifetime than most of the young New Left had dreamed of. He was a black man who exuded the mystery and vitality of the black race, and to young radicals, black experience was real and challenging. The young radicals who had worked with the movement for racial equality in the South recalled with envy the sense of community, the music and laughter of the black people they had met. Even the word hippie had originally come from the black slang for whites who sought out black people and took pleasure in their company. In the sixties, thousands of Americans joined the original hippies and imitated black language, lifestyle, music, food, and clothing.

George Jackson's *Soledad Brother* was the second black classic of the period. It was a collection of letters written from prison to his mother and others about his development as a revolutionary and as an individual. Jackson had been in and out of prison since he was a teen-ager. By the time he wrote the book he was in his mid-twenties and had educated himself by sheer will. Jackson was determined not to allow himself to be destroyed by racism or broken by white society.

He turned himself into a physically superb individual by discipline and constant exercise—he said he was preparing his body for the revolution. He read deeply in revolutionary literature—Lenin, Marx, Frantz Fanon, *The Autobiography of Malcolm X*—and developed his own individual version of a revolt that would free black people from the position they held in society. Jackson was killed during a prison riot at Soledad in 1971 and was mourned by the Black Panthers as the greatest of black revolutionary writers.

Finally, the American Indian followed the black as a revolutionary hero and symbol of the New Left. Young Indians became active on their own, demanding improvement of reservations and living conditions. White radicals joined them and pointed out that the Indian had been the earliest victim of American aggression and greed. The New Left argued that America had been founded upon genocide, upon the destruction of the Indian races so that the white man could occupy the land.

The second general group of idols and heroes held in esteem by the New Left were underground figures and others involved in questioning the values of modern, affluent society. These individuals were rarely revolutionary in the sense that Che or Mao were; they tended to be revolutionary in a deeper and more radical sense. They were spiritual and emotional rebels who rarely found satisfaction in politics; they were individualistic, and sought a society in which they could preserve their individualities and spiritual freedoms.

First among these underground and literary heroes was the poet Allen Ginsberg. Ginsberg was part of the Beat Generation, a group of nonconformist writers and artists of the fifties who were among the first to challenge American ideals and customs following World War II. Ginsberg remained influential and important in the sixties and was the only person to bridge the gap between Beat and New Left, between hippie and politically committed. He had friends who were mystics; he knew Bob Dylan, Hell's Angels, New York intellectuals, and European poets. Ginsberg was more a religious person than a political revolutionary, and his importance to the New Left came from his deep commitment to experimentation and truth and his search for basic values and meaning in life. He frequently served as a moderating and quieting influence among factions of radicals. Often he brought heated emotions to calm by chanting Hindu mantras and Holy Songs and by reminding his listeners that all life is holy and valuable.

For a while, Timothy Leary, a one-time Harvard professor, was a hero of young radicalism. He had been imprisoned on charges of possessing marijuana and LSD and freed secretly by members of the Weatherman organization, a radical offshoot of the Students for a Democratic Society. *The Politics of Ecstasy* was Leary's attempt to convert revolutionaries to LSD. The book maintained that basic change in thinking and society could come only through drugs. Only a few were moved by Leary's arguments. To the many other young radicals who had seen friends destroyed by excessive use of LSD, Leary's book was not convincing. Leary has been living in exile, moving from country to country. He was driven from Algeria at Eldridge Cleaver's insistence. Close contact with Leary had convinced Cleaver that Leary was not truly revolutionary and was dangerous to the cause. Leary attempted to find a home in Switzerland, but was told to leave by government officials. He has now returned to the United States and is serving his sentence for drug possession at San Quentin Prison in California.

Another of these underground figures was the novelist Norman Mailer. Mailer was a peripheral figure and not in the mainstream of New Left development. But he is important because he became one of the most familiar faces at New Left rallies and demonstrations and because his writing in the sixties reflected the attitudes of many young radicals. Mailer had written the best of all essays on rebellion in modern America—"The White Negro" (1957)—and had anticipated the style and philosophy of the New Left. During the sixties, he published two works—*Why We Are In Vietnam?* and *The Armies of the Night*—which were read by many students interested in the new politics.

Several other writers should be mentioned as heroes of the new radicalism. Albert Camus, a Frenchman from Algeria, was an author who had been read by many young people who had worked in the South. Camus urged his readers to have moral commitment in what he called an "absurd world." Jean-Paul Sartre, another Frenchman, was widely read and discussed. The German author, Gunther Grass, provided good advice and aid to the New Left of his country. Grass reminded the young German radicals of the mistakes made by extremists in earlier leftist movements and urged the German New Left to temper its demands with a sense of what was possible and obtainable. These writers were international favorites and were known in Japan and America, as well as in Europe.

The nonliterary art of the young radical movement was limited to posters, music, and film. The posters of Mao Tse-tung, Che Guevara, and other radical figures have already been mentioned; also widespread, however, were posters advocating the different causes of the New Left. Often these posters were clever and interesting, and called for "Peace, Now!" or argued that "War is not healthy for children and other living things." Some posters were more heavily satirical and some even vicious. They accused America and its president of genocide and other evil acts.

Protest songs and folk songs were the music of the early New Left. Such songs had been sung by the activists in the South during the first part of the decade. "We Shall Overcome" was heard everywhere and was later quoted by President Johnson in a speech to a joint session of Congress on equal rights legislation. Popular too were "Negro spirituals" and other folk songs that spoke of the centuries of slavery and oppression; black singers such as Odetta and Leadbelly became best sellers.

But the first original songs to make an impression on radicalism, however, were those of Bob Dylan. Dylan combined a fine gift for words and songs with a talent for publicity and image-making. He established a legend around himself that was only partly true, but which places him among the idols of the New Left movement, as well as among its artists. It was told that Dylan had run away from home several times as a child and that he left the University of Minnesota as a freshman. He was said to have preferred freedom and to have wandered throughout the country, singing for his room and board and meeting legendary figures such as Woody Guthrie, the folk singer who had written "This Land Is Your Land."

The truth was that Dylan headed rather quickly for New York after leaving Minnesota and in a comparatively short time made himself famous and wealthy. In the early sixties, he had gone South for a while with civil rights workers and had sung songs with black musicians in Mississippi. By 1964, he had written many songs, three of which became classics in the early radical movement—"Blowin' in the Wind," "Masters of War," and "The Times, They Are a Changin'." After a bad motorcycle accident in the mid-sixties, Dylan retreated into isolation. His days of political activism were over, but the influence of his music lasted through the decade. He helped to raise the "political consciousness" of many young men and women.

Joan Baez, a less creative talent than Dylan, became the great heroine of the early movement. Her records of folk songs sold in great numbers, and her dark, striking looks became well known in civil rights activities, the antiwar cause, and the Free Speech Movement at Berkeley. As the sixties wore on she became less prominent, for her devotion to nonviolence kept her away from the more extreme and violent wing of the New Left.

The great English groups likewise joined the New Left. The Beatles started their career by singing standard ballads of love, but found themselves growing more political after 1966. John Lennon became particularly involved in the antiwar movement with his wife, Yoko Ono, but all four Beatles sang songs of protest and social commentary.

The Beatles were quickly followed into radicalism by the Rolling Stones. The Stones' lifestyles and actions had always been more violent and rebellious than those of the

Beatles; many people who found Lennon and his group acceptable were frightened by the raw energy of the Stones. "I Can't Get No Satisfaction" and "Street Fightin' Man" were among the most challenging and revolutionary songs of the decade. Hosts of other groups came and went—Peter, Paul and Mary, The Fugs, The Doors, The Jefferson Airplane—but none had the influence or popularity of the Stones, the Beatles, or Dylan.

The film of the New Left found its highest and most significant development in the work of the French director Jean-Luc Godard. Godard's films have been seen the world over and have been part of the international background shared by the New Left movements of various nations. Godard called himself a radical and supported the student rebels of France. He walked out of a film festival, which he found too capitalistic and middle class. His films are often about the New Left and, in one, he anticipated the movement of the New Left toward terrorism. *La Chinoise* was made before the revolution of 1968 and was about a small group of Maoist students who plan and carry out assassinations. We learn much from the film about the young New Left in France, for we live with them from day to day, listen to their talk, and join them on their terrorist acts.

Other Godard films likewise pictured young radicals in action. *Weekend* showed a group of young guerrilla fighters in rural France carrying on a war with the bourgeoisie and others who refused to join the revolution. *One Plus One* used the Rolling Stones as they made a record as background for a broad presentation of New Left revolutionary aims. As the Stones sing various versions of a song before reaching a final and satisfactory one, Black Panthers and other revolutionaries read their manifestoes and speak generally about their goals and desires.

The heroes, music, and film of the new radicalism were the most dynamic and best-known part of the movement. What the radicals expressed in their songs and in their devotion to Che Guevara and Eldridge Cleaver provides the best key to understanding what the New Left was all about. But there was also a deeper, more thoughtful side to the New Left, and this side is reflected in the thinkers and writers who wrote in their articles and books precisely what it was that disgusted them about American society and modern civilization. They also described methods of changing society and elaborated on the sort of society they would like to see follow the collapse of the present-day structure.

We shall describe the writings of six of these New Left thinkers. Two of them are members of an older generation; two are between youth and middle age; and two are young men who were very much a part of New Left activity. The six have much in common with one another in spite of the differences in age, and each has added his own particular way of thinking to the development of New Left radicalism.

The man who did more than any other to develop the thinking of the New Left in America and to predict its coming was the social critic Paul Goodman. Goodman, who was born in New York City in 1910 and died during the summer of 1972, devoted a lifetime to analyzing America's ills and proposing solutions. He styled himself a "neolithic conservative," by which he meant he feared government, and looked for simple solutions to problems. For Goodman, all the money and power invested in Washington had solved little; he felt that people at the local level, in small groups, could best handle their own grievances and needs.

Goodman himself lived a simple life, without much money. He wrote well about a number of problems from the New Left movement itself to the evils that technology had brought mankind. About the New Left, Goodman said that he was at first happy to see youth concerned with injustice and social change, but was later chagrined by their extremism. He added that the sons proved no better than the fathers and that he was frightened by the moral self-righteousness and violence that proceeded from much New Left activity.

Of technology, Goodman wrote that it had been a mixed blessing. It made life easier for millions and, for that reason, was good. But it had likewise made war more efficient and was destroying the environment. Instead of fleeing from the modern world with the hippies, it was necessary for man to learn how to control his technology so that it was used only for his improvement.

Goodman's deepest and most important study of American life, however, was his analysis of its educational system. His classic work on this subject was *Growing Up Absurd,* which he first published in 1956. The work was subtitled "Problems of Youth in the Organized Society." It was Goodman's idea that thousands of young people were growing up in America with no sense of community, common interest, or values. These young men and women were the result of a system that was becoming more and more organized to produce individuals who would keep the system going. Little attention was paid to the young outside of the need to produce and manufacture them for the system.

Goodman asked two difficult and important questions. First, he asked what sort of society was it that the young were being asked to become a part of and, second, he asked if there wasn't much about American society that was inhumane, unnatural, and worthless. Goodman was arguing that people should stop and ask, do we have the right to force boys and girls into a society that is unhealthy and destructive? and he was answering, no, we do not have that right.

The United States, Goodman continued, was often deficient in conditions that permitted the young to grow up in physical and emotional health, for America was committed to competition, to the isolation of individual from individual, and to values that destroyed true community, patriotism, and honor. America would pay for her poor educational system, Goodman warned, for a whole generation would grow up to be wild, without values, and would need to search for them. This search would lead to delinquency, violence, and other forms of rebellion. The young of the New Left were among the rebels that Goodman prophesied; they were part of the generation "growing up absurd."

The second figure of New Left thought from an older generation is Herbert Marcuse (pronounced Mar-cooz-ah). Marcuse was a German citizen who came to the United States to escape Hitler's Reich. His lifelong interest has been social analysis, and he has been a productive writer and teacher. His most important works are *Eros and Civilization* (1955) and *One-Dimensional Man* (1964). His best-known student to date has been Angela Davis, a young black communist professor who has played an important role in the American left.

Marcuse is an academic person; he is scholarly and quiet. His criticism of modern, industrial society is careful and learned. At times he is difficult to understand because his writing becomes bogged down in language that is too scholarly. But at times his social criticism is on-target and devastating. Marcuse argues that Western society—the society of those countries that are wealthy and developed—has created a new kind of tyranny and social control. Instead of using terror and physical pain to keep people from rebelling and opposing the government, modern nations keep their citizens well-fed, well-clothed, and well-housed. All opposition and criticism are swallowed up by the advance of technology and the increase of wealth.

Western society is a society without opposition, one where people are materially and physically content. But Marcuse argues that these advanced countries have created "one-dimensional men" in one-dimensional societies. Material satisfaction is not happiness, and it is not freedom. Industrial society, in providing all the goods and services that men need, fails to provide spiritual values and the freedom to develop the full range of human possibility. In modern society, man is unable to enjoy the work he does, for it is too easy, too abstract, and too technical. It is not done with the hands and the heart. Likewise, modern man has no meaningful leisure and has lost the ability to enjoy company, love, and life in general.

What is more, Marcuse argues, is that modern society has built within itself the very means to prevent its own change and improvement in quality. Marcuse's logic runs like this. He describes how the United States had become involved in the cold war. The threat of communism had caused America to increase military and industrial output tremendously. The country had grown wealthy, and with it the nations of Europe and Japan. But America became a victim of its own cold war: Americans found they couldn't abandon the war because industry would decline, salaries would shrink, and prosperity would be no more. For the sake of more TV sets and refrigerators, Marcuse says, America and the West will go on making bombs and will not make the social changes necessary to end the threat of war and improve the condition of man's soul.

What is Marcuse's solution to the dilemma of modern man? Marcuse wants a revolution that encompasses the whole man, and it is here that he emerges as perhaps the most revolutionary and visionary of New Left writers. He wants a restructuring of society that would give modern man more true leisure and would reestablish a sense of pride and value in the work men do. Marcuse wants an end to consumer society with its ever-increasing number of goods that people don't need. If these changes are made, then the natural health of man will return and he will lose the frustration caused by modern living. Technology and society must work for people, not people for technology and society.

Regis Debray and Frantz Fanon were younger and much angrier than Goodman or Marcuse when they wrote the books that made them prominent in the New Left. Debray is hardly a household name, but he has proved to be one of the most significant and important figures in the New Left. His works are read in Berlin, Paris, and Chicago by all those interested in making a revolution work.

Debray is a Frenchman who left France in the early sixties because he found the leftists of his home country hopelessly divided and too full of talk. He chose to go to Latin America, where things were happening, to observe the left as it faced day-to-day problems of survival and warfare. Debray visited guerrillas in Columbia, Venezuela, Brazil and other countries in South America. He joined Che and Castro in Cuba and later went to Bolivia to fight with Che and his followers there; before Che died, he wrote in his diary that Debray was a brave, admirable man. The Bolivians captured Debray and imprisoned him for several months. He has now returned to France, but his travels keep him in contact with revolutionaries throughout the world.

Among Debray's works, two stand out as central and most important. These are the long essay entitled "Castroism: The Long March in Latin America," and the short book

*Revolution in the Revolution?*. Debray demands total commitment to revolution now. The first and foremost duty of a revolutionary is to make a revolution. Through his experience and work, Debray sought the most efficient means to change society, and he came to the conclusion that this means would be violent. He told his readers that innocent victims would be killed on both sides and that they would have to choose which side they would fight for.

Revolution can be brought about by the *foco,* Debray argued. By a *foco,* he meant a center, or focus, of revolutionary activity. A group of radicals could create a *foco* by concentrating on the weakest links of society. Castro and Che had fought for years in the jungles of Cuba against the weakest links of the Battista government. They had been successful, because they had concentrated on minor, day-to-day realities, such as food for their *foco,* weapons, and clothing, and had likewise appealed to the deepest sympathies of the Spanish-speaking people.

The *foco* is created by a group of dedicated men, but these men cannot themselves seize power. Their work is meant to help the masses overthrow the established government. The *foco* is the center of revolutionary activity directed to the interests of the people; it educates the people in revolution and gives the people repeated examples of heroism and courage. The *foco,* or guerrilla force, is to be the small motor that sets the large motor of the masses in motion.

One necessary center of *foco* activity, according to Debray, was the university, for students are easily radicalized and their support is needed if a revolution is to succeed. It would be the radical young who would have the time and energy to carry the revolution to the masses of people. The young radicals who planned the insurrections at Columbia, Berlin, and Paris had read and absorbed Debray; they saw themselves as creating "one, two, three or more Vietnams," which would help bring America to its knees. The Weathermen, an extremist group, likewise styled itself into a *foco*-like group and tried to attack America at its "weakest links." Debray might have approved its revolutionary zeal, but would have added that the *foco* was primarily a method of carrying revolution to the peasants and only secondarily a means of bringing it to the university.

If Regis Debray can be considered the strategist of the revolution, Frantz Fanon is its psychologist. Born in Martinique, a French island in the Caribbean, and educated in France, Fanon came into contact with revolution in Algeria at the time of its struggle with France for independence. He lived and worked with Algerian revolutionaries and became very sympathetic with their problems and with the problems of all colonial peoples struggling for dignity and self-determination. Fanon used his psychological training to analyze the effects of colonialization and slavery on the peoples of Algeria and upon Africa as a whole. In his most important work, *The Wretched of the Earth* (1961), he spoke of the emotional harm done to generations of Africans by the white European conqueror. Many Africans, he argued, believed Europeans superior because the Europeans had subjugated and ruled the nations of Africa for many years. It was natural that a conquered people took on the myths and mentality of those who subjugated them. The Africans had come to believe themselves inferior because the white man told them so every day in a thousand different ways. Natives were separated from the Europeans who ruled and were not allowed to mix with them except as servants. Natives did menial work: cleaned house, carried heavy loads, or worked the fields. During the colonial period, everyone believed that the white rulers were enlightened, honest, and good, while the colored subjects were untrustworthy, shifty, and lazy.

This colonial mentality changed rapidly when colonialism ended. Revolution took place in the minds of natives when the whites withdrew from Africa. Violence, which had been kept under control for decades through fear and nonpolitical expression such as dance, was now breaking out all over. Fanon welcomed the violence and wrote that it was absolutely necessary. Violence restored people to mental and emotional health. It allowed the expression of deep-seated feelings, which had been pent up for years. Furthermore, violence made men of those who were violent. The African who had for centuries been the one who was beaten and enslaved could now prove himself through violence.

Fanon never explained why he felt that violence was evil when done by whites but good and necessary when done by other races. It was enough that the immediate effects of violence were good for the violent.

According to Fanon, violence does more than restore health and manhood; it develops a sense of community and common purpose, and this was to be its final contribution to the Third World. Those revolutionaries who arose and overthrew the white man would share a common experience that would unite them and forge them into a nation. Fanon lauded the spontaneous revolutionary act, for he felt that the more spontaneous an act, the healthier it was: the gangster who killed five or six policemen before being killed himself was a hero. It would be the gangsters of the world, the poor, the dispossessed, the alienated, who would make the revolution successful. The New Left used Fanon to justify its spontaneity and its turn to terrorism; Fanon also aided young radicals in their need to understand Third World problems and grievances. No work has been written with greater bitterness than Fanon's classic.

Tom Hayden has been to the New Left in America what Regis Debray was to the leftist movement in Latin America. Hayden has watched the New Left closely, examining its successes and failures and developing its theory. He speaks frequently on university and college campuses and has published many articles and several books on his views and experiences. His early articles appear in the important radical magazines *Liberation* and *Dissent.* Two of his books have been *Rebellion in Newark* (1967), which tells the story of the Newark riots of 1967, and *Trial* (1970), which is about his experiences as one of the "Chicago Seven," the group of prominent radicals tried for their participation in the demonstrations and protests at the Democratic Party Convention of 1968 in Chicago.

Hayden shares with Debray a concern that things happen. The first and primary goal of the revolutionary is to go among the poor and powerless. The poor and powerless realize they get a "raw deal" from society and are therefore potential revolutionaries. Yet Hayden knows the poor well enough to know that they are basically conservative, since they most often take their condition to be the way things have to be. The poor accept the wealthy's attitude toward them—that they are at the bottom because they're lazy, dumb, and incompetent. Furthermore, the poor are kept dependent upon the rich for jobs, salaries, housing, and food.

What can a leftist do to put an end to this? He can help the poor overcome their sense of fear and embarrassment before the rich and powerful. He can help the poor, both white and black, gain a sense of pride and self-worth. The revolutionary does this, says Hayden, by first of all involving himself in the day-to-day problems of the poor and winning such improvements as lower rents, better garbage collection, and more repairs on slum tenements. If the revolutionary is successful in these efforts, he will win the loyalty of the poor and instill in them a feeling that they can make decisions that will affect their lives. This is the participatory democracy Hayden longs for—a return to the democracy of nineteenth-century America, where local areas took care of local problems.

Hayden recognized early the importance of the student movement. He wrote of young, affluent Americans who were uninterested in careers and money and more concerned with social change and justice. These young people, Hayden said, were clumsy when it came to ghetto work, for they were of another world—overeducated, rich, and respectable. Yet Hayden argued that the students were needed, that their energy and commitment could be used. Hayden said that students and the poor helped one another to feel real: students needed the experience of living among the powerless; the poor needed the energy of the students, for the students brought to the ghetto the feeling that change can happen. Hayden's final goal for society was the final goal of all New Left writers: to restore meaning and humanity to a system they feel has become too gigantic, too militaristic, and too authoritarian.

The final writer that we will discuss is Daniel Cohn-Bendit, the leader of the French student insurrection. Cohn-Bendit is the son of German-Jewish parents and a German citizen. He provides a link between the New Lefts of France and Germany. Following the "May Days" of 1968, he and his wife, Gabrielle, wrote a book entitled *Obsolete Communism: The Left-Wing Alternative,* which discusses what had happened in May and the goals of the French New Left in general.

The Cohn-Bendits are adamant in their rejection of bureaucracy, whether it be Russian, American, or French. They argue that modern society has created a whole new class of managers—the bureaucrats—and that these bureaucrats are increasing their power day by day. There is some agreement between the bureaucrat and the capitalist wealthy class, but this agreement is not final, for the bureaucracy has become a power unto itself, unresponsive to the demands of the rest of society.

This bureaucracy has meant the end of democracy, though it has continued to pay lip service to democracy and to claim that it acts in the name of democracy. For the Cohn-Bendits, France, the United States, and the Soviet Union have become states where the real decisions are made by the few people high up in the bureaucracy. Voting by the masses is simply a means of ratifying what has already been decided. There is no real decision for the people to make. There is no real democracy.

The revolution must concentrate on ending this bureaucracy and returning power to the people. Thus the Cohn-Bendits share common goals with Debray and Hayden. They are more extreme than Debray, however, and demand that the revolution have *no leaders,* for leaders mean a return to decision from above. Cohn-Bendit condemns Lenin for being another bureaucrat; he accuses Lenin of fearing the people, refusing to listen to them, and of forming a party where decisions were made by the few for the many.

The great moment of the May Days of 1968 for the Cohn-Bendits came when there was a temporary withering of power and disappearance of state, university, and labor union. For a while each interest group—students, workers, shopkeepers, and so on—concentrated on its own problems, without outside interference. For a while new relationships among people and groups were established and society seemed on the road to change.

But then the power of the police, combined with the lack of interest of the workers (once they had achieved their goals of fewer working hours and better conditions), put an end to the revolution. The society the Cohn-Bendits desire would be diverse and would have no hierarchy; there would be no racism and no distinctions due to wealth or sex. Finally, technology would benefit all people and there would no longer be those who must renounce and sacrifice because of their poverty while others enjoy life because of their wealth.

From Che Guevara to Daniel Cohn-Bendit, the heroes and thinkers of the new radicalism share common goals and themes. They attack modern civilization for its unjust use of power and force and demand that reform take place in society so that power and force will be used more wisely and beneficially. They seek government that will be sensitive to the people and a people that can govern themselves without outside interference or dictation from above. All condemn bigness as destructive of basic human values.

What made the New Left distinctive in the sixties was that it renewed the call made by others in the past to improve the quality of life. In countries where the basic needs of life were no longer a problem for the majority of people, the New Left sought a revolution in the realm of excellence. They wanted to improve the lot of the poor, but they likewise insisted that the poor be more than fed and housed. They wanted to make education not just adequate, but meaningful. They wanted men to take pride once again in their work, their leisure, and their society.

Youth movements have traditionally sought such goals and have worked for the improvement of quality as well as the satisfaction of basic needs. Now that we have taken a look at the art and thought of the New Left, it is time to examine its history and trace its evolution, activity, and fate in the affluent countries of the world. The story of its deeds and accomplishments has both a hopeful and a tragic side. What started out as an idealistic effort to change the way men think and act often ended by being an effort to force men to behave in preconceived kinds of behavior and to conform to some unattainable and undesirable pattern of justice. Youthful reform movements often begin with a hopeful message to deliver to mankind and end in frustration, despair, and unhappiness for many of those involved.

# THE EARLY NEW LEFT IN AMERICA: FROM GREENSBORO THROUGH BERKELEY

Some writers and political observers in the 1950s announced that radicalism had come to an end in the United States. The Old Left had been discredited by the ruthlessness of Stalin, and only a few die-hard communists still maintained that the Soviet Union was a just and free society. On the campuses, there were no radical organizations, and the vast majority of students displayed little interest in politics. Student energy and aggression were vented on sports and fraternities. A few professors spoke out against the apathy of their students and wondered what would become of America when this spiritless group of young people, later called the "silent generation," assumed power.

Student apathy and disinterest, however, did not reflect the deeper problems of the period. America was growing more wealthy and better fed during the seeming calm and quiet of the Eisenhower administration, but many people were bothered by problems that had nothing to do with money or their stomachs. Russia now had the atomic bomb, and all mankind was threatened by a war between communism and democracy. The cold war meant more jobs for Americans in weapon factories, but it also added to insecurity and nervous strain at the same time. What was the importance of more jobs and better salaries, if everyone could be blown to pieces at any time?

Politics in the fifties had been changed by the protracted cold war with communism. Senator Joseph McCarthy of Wisconsin had uncovered a few former communists in government and had accused many others of being communist sympathizers. Through a skillful use of innuendo he succeeded, almost singlehandedly, in creating a witch-hunt environment. Out of fear for their jobs and families, few wanted to be identified with a radical, or even a liberal, past. In this atmosphere, it is not surprising that radicalism seemed to disappear.

Two new and important movements appeared in the fifties, however, and were able to survive the cold war and the growth of American affluence and power. The first movement that was to prove influential was begun by a small group of young people called Beatniks or the Beat Generation, who rejected wealth and affluence, and who had no sympathy for America's war against communism. The second significant social movement of the period was the major upheaval set in motion by the Supreme Court school desegregation decision of 1954.

Beatniks began to appear in large American cities, particularly San Francisco and New York, in the late forties and early fifties. They refused to work at regular jobs and lived lives unhampered by the problems they saw destroying thousands of Americans. Above all, they emphasized freedom and the right of each individual to choose his way of personal expression. They found their heroes among society's rejected: the black, the hobo, the eccentric, and the junkie. They found the poor and powerless more admirable than the rich and hard-working.

Two men emerged as the principal spokesmen of the Beatnik movement. The first was a poet from New Jersey, Allen Ginsberg, whose "Howl" (1956) summed up all the disgust and hatred the Beat felt for American society. Jack Kerouac, the second, wrote a novel *On the Road* (1957) that became an underground classic in the late fifties and early sixties. Both Ginsberg and Kerouac repudiated wealth and success and asked their followers to turn their backs on material goods such as split-level homes, good jobs, and cars. As alternatives to material goods they stressed feeling and love and asked Americans to return to nature, to enjoy beauty and simplicity. Many of these values were later to be at the core of New Left thought in the sixties.

A more significant change in American society was brought about by the Court order to desegregate schools. Emancipation of the American Negro had taken place nearly a hundred years earlier, but black citizens had been suppressed into second-class positions in every aspect of political and social life. Some people had attempted change before 1954, but the vast majority of Americans seemed indifferent, if not hostile, to the civil rights of minorities. The effort to establish the black as equal to the white meant a social revolution of great proportions that threatened to undo the calm and apathy of the period.

A hint of how greatly the calm could be undone by the new movement was given by the Montgomery, Alabama, bus boycott of late 1955. The boycott began when Mrs. Rosa Parks, a black woman, refused to give up her seat to a white man and move to the rear of the bus, the area designated for black people. The bus company, which followed the segregated customs of the South, did not support Mrs. Parks's right to sit wherever she wanted. Blacks throughout the city joined her protest, and for 381 days they refused to buy tickets on public transportation. The incident brought about an examination of segregation laws, and eventually led to the declaration by a federal court that racial laws were illegal when applied to bus transportation. Blacks had learned for the first time that they could successfully challenge the white power structure by working and organizing on their own, without the help of powerful liberal whites from the North.

By the early 1960s, small student groups of blacks and whites were discussing the issues raised by the Beat Generation and by the drive for civil rights. To these young people, it was apparent that changes had to be made in American society, and that the country had to be brought back to its original ideals of justice for all. In these early discussions, two primary problems were raised: first and foremost, the problem of how to improve the lot of the poor and powerless, particularly the black of the South, and second, the issue of university reform and the improvement of education.

Talk and discussion were easy, however, and thousands of young people looked for action and commitment to prove their sincerity. The opportunity came early in 1960. Four black students at the North Carolina Agricultural and Technical College in Greensboro decided to challenge the racial segregation laws and customs of their state. They had come to their decision alone and had no connection with a national organization. They resolved to "sit-in" at the lunch counter of the local F. W. Woolworth Company. Blacks had been permitted to enter the store and purchase articles, but were not allowed to sit at the store's lunch counter. The four students had their first "sit-in" on February 1; they demanded coffee and were told to leave. They remained at the counter until the store closed. It is from this date that most commentators trace the beginning of the New Left.

The next day, they were joined by other black students, and on the following day by several whites. By the end of the month, the whole South was involved in the sit-in movement. White racists heckled and often attacked the brave few who challenged the existing conditions. By the end of the year, an estimated 50,000 people had participated in some kind of protest in many cities, and over 3,600 had spent some time in jail for disrupting local customs and laws.

This early movement was inspired deeply by religion and by patriotism. Under the leadership of Dr. Martin Luther King, Jr., and other devout Christians, the cause of black equality took on a moral and religious aura, and Americans were reminded that all people are the Children of God. Likewise, the early demonstrators believed in the truth of the American Ideal, that all men are created equal, and endowed with inalienable rights. Optimistically, they felt that America could be changed if her conscience were awakened and challenged, if she were made aware of her shortcomings.

It did not take long for northern university students to become involved in the cause. What had been isolated discussion groups, quickly turned into a nationwide movement. Students from Hunter, Yale, Minnesota, Berkeley, Rutgers and elsewhere held marches in support of the sit-ins. Money was collected and sent south to help pay bail and other expenses. Busloads of young people went South on "Freedom Rides" to protest firsthand against racism and the segregation of transportation facilities. The Congress of Racial Equality (CORE) and Martin Luther King's Southern Christian Leadership Conference (SCLC) began to establish schools in nonviolent confrontation and civil disobedience, preparing for mass demonstrations.

Throughout the country, young men and women began planning to "go to the people," and work for the improvement of racial relations. Sit-ins and other demonstrations were not enough; work had to be done in education, voter registration, and in many other difficult and tedious areas. The first organization of the sixties to address itself to these mundane problems was the Student Nonviolent Coordinating Committee (SNCC, called "Snick").

SNCC represented the earliest actual appearance of the New Left. It was established in 1960 to organize the numerous white and black civil rights workers who had gone to work with the people of the South. It wanted to bring thousands of blacks into full citizenship by educating them in their rights as Americans, and by urging them to vote for the first time in their lives.

SNCC began establishing projects throughout the South. Volunteers worked in Alabama, Georgia, South Carolina, and elsewhere. Running into local white opposition, thousands of young people were beaten and arrested. Hoses were turned on them and dogs were set on them, but seldom did they stray from their commitment to nonviolence. Perhaps the single most outstanding example of courage in a courageous movement was when a young man named

Bob Parris went alone into the most backward and racist section of the South, Amite County, Mississippi, to help organize his fellow blacks and give them a voice in county politics.

The work and struggle of the volunteers in the South was brought to the attention of the whole nation by the march on Washington of 1963. Thousands of Americans, white and black, travelled to the capital to show support for equal rights and urge the passage of federal laws which would make discrimination because of race illegal. Martin Luther King made the most famous and stirring speech of his career as he spoke of the dream he had that all Americans could live together in love, peace, and brotherhood.

A major project was planned for the summer of 1964, when thousands of volunteers from northern and western colleges would spend their summer vacations working for SNCC. The Summer Project was to be a heavily organized and financed onslaught against racism and inequality. During the winter of 1963–64, SNCC gathered as many workers as it could.

The summer proved to be a central experience in the lives of many young radicals. They encountered firsthand the evils of American society and the difficulties of change and reform. Three young workers, two white and one black, were murdered in Mississippi and their bodies thrown into a dam construction site. No one was ever convicted for these murders.

Further frustration and failure followed. White legislatures gerrymandered political districts to destroy the effect in elections of newly registered blacks. A delegation of blacks chosen to represent Mississippi at the Democratic National Convention of 1964 was unsuccessful in obtaining its seats; the Democrats continued to honor the all-white delegation. In Georgia, the state legislature refused to allow a young black SNCC worker, Julian Bond, to take the seat he had won, because they said Bond's opposition to the Vietnam War was treasonous. The young politician took his case to court and won his right to become a legislator, but only after several years of legal difficulty and dispute.

During the spring of 1965, SNCC worked with other civil

rights organizations to plan the Selma to Montgomery, Alabama, march, only to meet with more frustration and failure. Volunteers were killed on the streets of large Alabama cities; a housewife volunteer from Detroit was found dead along a country road. The federal government seemed reluctant to investigate the crimes or to insure the safety of the workers. In the face of this partial defeat and setback, SNCC began to change and grow more radical. Factions divided the organization, as the followers of Bob Parris decided on one type of activity, and others decided on other plans of action.

In May 1966, militants under Stokely Carmichael, a young black from New York, carried the day. Carmichael and his followers spoke of a need for black people to solve their own problems and rejected the idea that blacks wanted to participate in the "American Dream." Carmichael denied being a racist or a black supremist; he simply argued that political power would come from somewhere other than the ballot box; black people would have to establish separate black political and cultural institutions. The new SNCC issued a manifesto setting forth these radical aims.

Carmichael's leadership radicalized SNCC and made it the first New Left organization to move to the extreme positions that would be held by young leftists in the later sixties. Indeed, Carmichael's move with SNCC had created the first truly revolutionary movement in America since the International Workers of the World, or "Wobblies," of the early part of the century. But Carmichael had done more; in addition to radicalizing SNCC, at the same time he had brought it outside of the New Left. Henceforth, blacks would be a part of "black liberation," a radical movement that has a history separate from that of the New Left and has striven for different goals. The separation of blacks and whites at the Columbia University insurrection underlined the separation of the two movements. Blacks had pride and identity to attain; whites were seeking more ambiguous goals.

It was the problems and frustrations encountered by SNCC in the South that helped form the personality and character of the New Left. Before going south, the students had only the vaguest notion of the social and political problems they would be facing; they desired justice and equality for the black man, but had no definite plan for achieving these ends. In contact with the realities of daily life in the South, the young radicals came to emphasize goals of community work, grass-roots participation, and pure democracy. They developed the technique of the peaceful demonstration later used in the large marches on Washington and elsewhere, and created the local organizing projects and centers that were to play such an important part in their concept of democracy. Even during periods of deep frustration and despair, they did not lose faith in their Jeffersonian belief that the people could take care of their own problems, given the chance. The radical SNCC manifesto expressed this idea when it concluded, "We reaffirm our belief that people who suffer must make the decisions about how to change and direct their lives."

The second New Left organization to come into being was the Students for a Democratic Society (SDS). SDS was founded by a group of northern university students who were among those to learn of politics from experience in the South. They had originally joined student organizations sponsored by the Old Left, but had quickly become disillusioned with the Old Left's constant talk and sparse action. The young radicals accused the Old Left of being afraid to take radical positions on social issues out of terror of being called communist. All of this, to the young, was a waste of time; the duty of the left was to make revolution, and not be fearful of name-calling.

Chief among the founding fathers of SDS was a young man from Detroit named Tom Hayden. Hayden had been editor of the daily paper at the University of Michigan and had been one of the earliest political activists. He had demonstrated at the Democratic National Convention of 1960 in Los Angeles. He had friends at Berkeley whom he visited, learning of radicalism there. He was among the earliest to work in the South; he spent his twenty-second birthday in jail, in Albany, Georgia.

Hayden and his friends had learned firsthand of the poverty and powerlessness of many Americans. They discussed the formation of a new organization among themselves, and communicated with other activists they had met or had heard of, trying to arouse interest in a new radical group that would attack the problems of the poor in both the North and South and among both white and black Americans. A series of meetings was held from late 1961 through the spring of 1962. By summer, the organization was ready to move.

To the founding convention in June, 1962, at Port Huron, Michigan, student radicals came from the University of Michigan, Oberlin, Johns Hopkins, Swarthmore, and Earlham. A few workers from SNCC were there as well as several independent individuals. The convention adopted a platform, which has come to be known as "The Port Huron Statement." It was not a final declaration of purpose, they announced, but was "a living document open to change with our times and experiences." By implication, if not outright declaration, the Port Huron Statement underlined the separation between the old and the new left. The young men and women who drew up the statement saw themselves as establishing a new, revitalized left, one that would be free of the mistakes of the old left and one that would not be subject to control by old left organizations.

The document outlined the grievances of its drafters. "Our work is guided by the sense that we may be the last generation in the experiment of living," they announced. If the bomb did not annihilate civilization, then tyrannical and authoritarian government, in both the East and the West, would turn mankind into puppets unwilling and unable to experiment or find new ways of living. To counteract this danger, the document argued, it was necessary to establish a sense of community and common interest. In America, competition, the drive "to get ahead," and the desire for more money had created a lonely, frustrated population who cared little about their fellow man. These people needed "participatory democracy," which would give them a new sense of responsibility and power. Participatory democracy was a system governed by two central aims: "that the individual share in those social conditions determining the quality and direction of his life," and, "that society be organized to encourage independence in men and provide the media for their common participation." The general direction of SDS was to be that of a catalyst, bringing people together at the local level to talk about and solve their own problems.

The document attacked the problems of education. The American university needed to be overhauled because it fostered irrelevant values and created apathy. The university could be the means of educating a new generation against social injustice and for participatory democracy. Radicals could use the universities as a means of spreading New Left ideas and gospel. Finally, the document concluded, "A new left must start controversy across the land, if national policies and national apathy are to be reversed. The ideal university is a community of controversy, within itself and in the effects on communities abroad."

In 1962, SDS had fifty members. Its early activities were necessarily modest—SDS delegates attended the National Student Association meeting of 1962 and began working in campus politics at several large universities. Over the next months, radical politics grew among the young as civil rights activities expanded. SDS took advantage of student interest, and by the end of the first year of its existence had over nine hundred members and had opened chapters at Yale, Harvard, Berkeley, and Michigan.

By 1966, the nine hundred had grown to an estimated 5,500 active members in 151 chapters in thirty-seven states. Projects had been established throughout the country to organize the poor. SDS students from Swarthmore founded the first such project at the nearby working-class community of Chester, Pennsylvania. Other centers were founded in Chicago, Cleveland, Baltimore, Oakland, Boston, and in Appalachia.

These projects were intended to make participatory democracy a reality and were designed to help organize white, and sometimes black, ghetto residents into effective political groups. The most successful was the Newark Community Union Project (called "Encup"), which saw to it that slum repairs were made and won more frequent garbage collection for the ghetto residents. Also, one of Encup's activists was elected to a committee overseeing Newark's war on poverty.

But the majority of SDS's work and effort failed. Then between 1962 and 1966, the organization became more radical. Some of SDS's radicalism came from its association with SNCC and from the deep respect white radicals felt for black radicalism. But the new extremism likewise sprang from frustration with community projects and the failure of participatory democracy to take hold.

The entire experience of the early New Left was not monopolized by SNCC and SDS, however. A third movement had begun on campuses and had little to do with the civil rights movement or the work of SDS in the ghettoes. This movement was the increasing demand among students for reform of the universities themselves.

University reform was a vague and less clear-cut cause than poverty or racism. There could be no definite program of action, such as voter registration, to pursue and act upon. Students complained about the size of the schools and about professors they never saw, but were uncertain about how to voice their grievances effectively. To many students, the schools had become nothing but machines, grinding out puppets for America's military and industrial complex. At the larger universities across the country demands for change had been made, but the schools had turned a deaf ear and continued to expand, enlarge classes, exempt professors from teaching duty and to add to the already massive administration and school bureaucracy.

Nowhere was the bureaucracy larger than at the University of California at Berkeley. Students at Berkeley were among the first in the nation to protest and make their complaints known during the late fifties and early sixties. They demanded the right to exercise a wide range of political beliefs and to invite speakers they wanted to lecture on campus. They asked that ROTC (Reserve Officers Training Corps) be voluntary and raised other issues involving the civil and political freedom of students.

This friction between the students at Berkeley and the university administration came to a head in the fall of 1964. The question at hand was somewhat complex. The university had traditionally allowed a section of the campus to be used as a "free-speech area," where people could speak on a variety of subjects, from vegetarianism to Mao Tse-tung.

There is a law in California that permits free speech, but that does not permit what it calls "advocacy." It is lawful to make a speech on communism, but it is unlawful *to advocate* communism, vegetarianism, or any other "ism." The distinction, of course, is a precious one, and impossible to make in reality. Up to 1964, the university had not pressed the issue of "advocacy" and had allowed almost anything to be said.

But the administration decided to enforce the law in the fall of 1964. Student activity was responsible for this change of policy. The numerous radicals who had spoken in the free-speech area earlier had not caused revolt or political activity. Now the administration was faced with a new generation of activists who had actually demonstrated against racism and other ills in San Francisco and the Bay Area and had raised the ire of many influential residents who wanted the activity stopped. The university, therefore, decided to act.

The administration had not reckoned, however, on the commitment of the radicals involved. Many were returning from SNCC's Summer Project in the Deep South and were now more thoroughly concerned with politics than ever. They became enraged over the university's attempt to limit their political activity on campus and stop the collecting of funds for radical work. The situation was further proof to them that the university was tyrannical, that it manipulated students and ordered them around with no consideration for their basic rights.

At first, only a few students placed themselves in confrontation with the school by using the free-speech area without a permit. When a few were suspended for their actions, larger numbers began to protest. On October 1, several thousand students surrounded a police car that held a young man arrested for "advocacy" and refused to allow the car to move. Mario Savio, a young graduate student in philosophy, emerged as the leader of this protest and became the best known of the Berkeley radicals. It was Savio, twenty-four at the time, who gained fame for his slogan, "trust no one over thirty."

The students agreed to cease their protests and demonstrations while a discussion was carried on with the administration. By November 9, however, the students grew suspicious of the administration's intentions, for no settlement seemed forthcoming. The Free Speech Movement, as it had come to be known, threatened to renew its activities, and on the next day, many were back at the free-speech area, setting up tables, and distributing information. For several weeks students and administration were at an impasse.

The Berkeley revolt quickly became known nationwide. Mario Savio and other leaders traveled to different campuses to gain support for the cause. Folk singer Joan Baez, joined the students and was a frequent leader of demonstrations, although she herself was not a student. One young man was widely reported in the press for carrying a poster saying, "I am a human being. Please do not fold, staple, bend, or mutilate."

By December 3, the patience of the university and the state of California had worn thin. Governor Edmund (Pat) Brown ordered the police to clear a building, Sproul Hall, the students had occupied. There were so many students within the hall that the task took the police twelve hours. Students were given time to leave the building before being arrested; when arrested, they were allowed to walk out of the building, or were dragged out. Most went limp and were dragged. It is difficult to say how many students were arrested; many gave false names or duplicated names of others. Altogether, however, there seems to have been at least seven hundred arrested.

The police invasion infuriated the students. The strike continued, and 5,000 students (Berkeley had a total student body of 17,500) listened to radical leaders denounce the university. On December 7, Savio was dragged from a platform by police when he attempted to speak, following a speech by the president of the university.

Student protest continued, but the outcome remained uncertain. Even when some order was restored to Berkeley by the beginning of the second semester, no one knew for sure who the victor was. Some short-term goals had been won by the students—a new head of the university was to be appointed and concessions on student political matters were made. The school announced a new liberal attitude toward free speech and advocacy, but the free-speech area remained basically under university supervision, and guest speakers still had to be approved by the administration. The students, however, had alienated the public at large. Few Californians sympathized with or understood the grievances. When a poll was taken, 55 percent of the state citizens who were polled "strongly disapproved" of what the radicals had done.

The Free Speech Movement brought to a close the early phase of the New Left in America. The character and nature of the movement was now open for all to see. In the South, in the ghettos, and at Berkeley, the New Left had shown that it preferred action above all else. Theory was something the Old Left could indulge in, young radicalism would move in and attack a problem directly, learning in the course of activity how to handle the situation. The Old Left wrote books and debated Marxist theory; the New Left moved into Newark or Chester, Pennsylvania, or took over Sproul Hall, and then learned in action about negotiating grievances and complaints.

Hand in hand with action, the New Left had proved that it preferred spontaneity. Instead of caution and forethought, it wanted to obey instinct and impulse. Spontaneity was preferred because it was honest and was unclouded by personal interest and hypocrisy. Spontaneity and action helped students overcome the boredom of classroom work and gave them something real and vital to do.

In addition, the early phase of the New Left had shown its deep and abiding commitment to democracy and early American ideals. Bigness and remoteness were opposed as evils of modern life, destroying democracy and making slaves of citizens. The young identified with the weak and powerless and wanted to rise to power with them. There was a strong conservative streak in New Left policy, a streak that was deeply opposed to the federal government and that believed that local government run by local people could best solve problems. The New Left often distrusted the power of Washington, as deeply as any conservative distrusted it.

It was this distrust of bigness that led the young radicals away from support of labor unions, the traditional area of leftist work and activity. In fact, the New Left has been unique among leftist movements in rejecting nearly all association with unions. The reasons for the rejection are easy to discover. Unions in the United States have been extraordinarily successful, many of them are rich, powerful institutions themselves. Students found them racist and conservative and argued that the unions were among the first things that would have to be changed following the revolution.

Less admirable characteristics of the New Left were also revealed in the early phase of its activity. A self-righteousness that bordered on fanaticism threatened to undo the good work that had been accomplished and to alienate people who might be attracted to the cause. What had begun a few years earlier as an effort to aid the poor and weak, became a movement that claimed to be the conscience of the nation, and sat in judgment of the strong, rich, and powerful.

Civil rights workers in the South had willingly accepted imprisonment, beatings, and even death as proof of their dedication and commitment. They had not asked to be above the law, or exempt from its cruelty. Yet students at Berkeley had demanded that those who broke university and state law be exonerated and not penalized. They considered themselves a moral force that could decide which laws were good and which bad, which laws they had to obey and which laws they could flout.

The self-righteousness of the students spread into other areas too. At Berkeley they refused to listen to opposing viewpoints, and although they gave lip service to tolerance and the right of all viewpoints to be heard, their preference for the left wing became obvious. The issue of free speech was not so clear-cut as the students presented it. There were genuine arguments on both sides. For the conservatives, unlimited free speech was potentially dangerous, for it permitted those who wanted to overthrow society to convert listeners to violence and extremism. For the sake of free speech, these conservatives asked, should the delicate balance of society be threatened? Could the state permit someone to speak when that person urged the murder of others or the destruction of their property? The radicals refused to see the problem in this light and said that any restriction on speech meant tyranny and authoritarianism.

In this self-righteousness and absolutism, the New Left had inherited the puritanic soul of many earlier American movements, from the sturdy, austere simplicity of the pilgrims to the fanaticism and arrogance of the abolitionists and prohibitionists. All these groups had refused to see shades of opinion. For them, as for many in the New Left, there was a right, and a wrong; there was nothing in between. A person could not compromise without destroying his soul.

Sociologists had begun to notice another trait of the New Left, that its membership was almost entirely young men and women from white, middle- and upper middle-class homes, most often families with a great deal of education. The young radicals were not the children of the Old Left, or of communists or socialists. Most often they were the children of moderately liberal professional people. Father was a doctor, dentist, university professor, or minister, and mother a college educated, social-minded woman who often immersed herself in community causes, or was herself a successful professional woman.

The young radicals, then, had enjoyed the best advantages of American life: suburban living, travel, education, and the benefits of pleasant homes, suitable clothing, and so on. They had been taught the best in the American political tradition—equality, the Bill of Rights, individual responsibility, and consideration for the underdog. It was therefore easy for them to be disillusioned when they found America falling short of her ideals, and it could be expected that they would feel guilt at having enjoyed lives that many Americans could not afford.

Kenneth Kenisten, a psychiatrist, has pointed out that the young members of the New Left, due to the affluence of their families, were permitted a protracted adolescence—a long period of "growing up" extended beyond the usual limits. When young working-class people were looking for jobs, marrying, and assuming the responsibilities of adult life, the new leftists were going to college, traveling, or enjoying some other benefit of family money. Family money likewise kept them free from summer jobs between college years, so they could work in ghettos and in the South.

Continued education allowed the affluent young to think more and more about society and to ponder deeply about personal problems and the problems of others. The vast majority of the new radical students were taking their major studies in literature or social science, not in science or engineering, and these liberal arts subjects stimulated their interest in social and individual improvement. Thus, avoiding the pitfalls and challenges of family and job responsibility, the young radicals found themselves concerned with a whole new set of problems such as, who am I? What is society, and what is justice? Having high opinions of their own personal worth, these young people preferred to devote themselves to "worthwhile" projects, and not waste themselves, as the Beatniks said, on the rat race.

The sociologist, Lewis Feuer, offered another reason for young radicalism. History has been full of generation rebelling against generation, he wrote. Sons have risen against fathers and have accused their fathers of tyranny, injustice, and corruption since the beginning of time. Plato and Aristotle recorded the problem in Ancient Greece, and countless other writers have discussed it. The rebellion of the sixties, the writer concluded, was simply another of these generational conflicts, a period when the young found it necessary to prove themselves a worthy generation by attacking the old.

All of these explanations have some truth in them, and the final reason for the revolt of the sixties is a combination of all. At any rate, the New Left had formed and made itself known; it was now ready to move into its second phase of development.

# THE SECOND PHASE: THE VIETNAM PROTEST, FROM TEACH-IN TO TERRORISM

Opposition to the war in Vietnam shaped New Left activity and policy during the second phase of its history. The war came to dominate the thinking of the young radicals so fully that earlier campaigns against racism and for the poor were abandoned or set aside. Peace was not a new cause, for statements had been issued from the beginning phases of the New Left against the testing of atomic bombs and against American military aid to right-wing nations. But Vietnam had hardly been noticed. It took the massive build-up of American troops in 1965 to bring opposition out in the open. SDS and other leftists seized upon the war to add to the vitality of the radical movement and to win further student support. Two tactics were employed in the early phase of opposition; the first was the "teach-in," the second, the march or demonstration.

The teach-in was simply an occasion when students and professors gathered, usually in large auditoriums or gymnasiums, to discuss the pros and cons of the war. Professors who had some knowledge of American foreign policy or some acquaintance with the problems and history of Southeast Asia would speak and attempt to give their listeners some perspective on the issues. What the organizers of the teach-ins hoped to do was to take discussion of the war away from the higher echelons of government. They were bringing participatory democracy to the campus and hoped that all Americans would follow the example and examine the war. The activists were weary of government officials and others who claimed that the average citizen did not know enough to make a wise judgment on Vietnam; the teach-ins were to prove that viable discussion could take place. The New Left felt that the war was too important to be left to the experts.

The first teach-in was held at the University of Michigan on March 24, 1965. Others followed throughout the country in the next few months; hardly a large university or a major college failed to organize one. The largest occurred at Berkeley on May 22, of the same year, and lasted thirty-six hours. Some 12,000 people listened to speeches by some of America's most talented men: I. F. Stone, the editor of one of the most important political journals of the country, *I. F. Stone's Weekly;* Isaac Deutscher, the biographer of Trotsky and Stalin; Staughton Lynd, a historian, Yale professor, and member of the New Left; and Norman Mailer, the well-known flamboyant novelist.

At the best of the teach-ins a broad spectrum of views was presented, from those who supported the government to those who most violently opposed it. Supporters of American policy pointed to commitments made to Vietnam and Southeast Asia; they argued that if America allowed South Vietnam to fall to communism, then the other countries of the area would likewise fall, like a series of dominoes. Critics of Vietnam included those who argued simply that it was folly for America to become involved in a land war in Asia where conditions were not at all to America's advantage.

The critics who spoke from the point of view of the New Left, however, attacked the war from a number of positions. They argued against American aggression and arrogance in attempting "to police the world." They demanded that America stop sending troops to every small country where communism seemed a threat; they wanted America to be less concerned with the security of American investment abroad and more concerned with the weak and needy of America.

Other new leftists questioned the constitutionality of the war and pointed out that Congress had not officially sanctioned the war, as required by the Constitution. These people accused the president of usurping too much power and of tending toward tyranny.

Extremists sided with the Vietcong itself, America's enemy in Vietnam, and condemned American wars against small, weak countries. These speakers sided with the impoverished people and revolutionaries of the Third World and were the most violently anti-American of the New Left. The most celebrated of speakers taking this position was Professor Eugene Genovese of Rutgers University. Professor Genovese is reported by some to have announced at a teach-in at Rutgers on April 23, 1965, that he welcomed a Vietcong victory. Immediately afterward, the wrath of conservative politicians descended upon him, and some demanded that the governor of New Jersey fire him. Richard Nixon, at the time a private citizen, wrote a letter to *The New York Times* in which he defended academic freedom, but went on to agree with those who wanted Genovese out of Rutgers. Nixon argued that academic freedom did not extend to support of the enemy during wartime. However, the governor of the state, Richard Hughes, refused to fire the professor.

Many teach-ins were valid experiences in democracy because many views were heard and tolerated. Many others, however, became highly emotional affairs where radical views came to dominate, and speakers advocating other positions or supporting the government were shouted down. The arrogance of the New Left was partially to blame, but the enormous arrogance of the federal government likewise contributed to the tension. Secretary of State Dean Rusk refused to talk about the war and condemned as gullible educated persons who believed America should not be in Vietnam. McGeorge Bundy and Walt Rostow, both advisers to President Johnson and heavily responsible for America's involvement in the war, refused when asked to confront debaters or answer questions put to them by teach-in speakers and audiences.

The teach-in movement succeeded in bringing a number of viewpoints before students and a few other citizens and in making debate on the war more acceptable and respectable. But it had settled nothing. In final analysis, the teach-ins raised tempers and blood pressure without offering any kind of active program to vent temper and anger against the war. The government remained as powerful as ever, and the war went on; another method of raising opposition would have to be used if the radicals were to bring the war to an end.

Young radicals had begun to "vote with their feet"—to march and demonstrate—almost at the same time they had begun the teach-ins. A group of young Maoist students, who called themselves M-2-M, or May 2nd Movement, marched against the war as early as May 2, 1964, but went largely unnoticed. During the winter of 1964–65, SDS and several other organizations began to plan for demonstrations in Washington and other large cities. Twenty-five thousand marched on the capital on April 17, 1965.

A National Coordinating Committee to End the War in Vietnam was formed and began outlining the "International Days of Protest" to be held in one hundred cities in October. Between January and November of 1965, the number of U.S. troops in Vietnam grew from 25,000 to well over 100,000; this gave a tremendous boost to the antiwar cause.

The "Days of Protest" were a success, and some 80,000 people demonstrated in various cities throughout the country. Although the protests had been arranged by a number of groups, including the Old Left, the New Left, older peace groups, and newly founded peace groups, the press gave SDS the entire credit for their organization. The attorney general and several senators demanded an investigation of the SDS, which they feared to be communist. Official distrust of SDS grew when Tom Hayden, its founder, and historian Staughton Lynd, an early member, traveled to Hanoi with Herbert Aptheker, a long-time member of the Communist party in America. Official distrust and condemnation, however, only added to the fame of the New Left, and more and more students joined the movement. After the visit to Hanoi, SDS issued a statement attacking the war and urging young men to refuse service in the armed forces.

Nineteen sixty-six and early 1967 were spent in organization and grass-roots education. SDS and the other antiwar groups concentrated on forming a larger popular base for the movement. This work was successful, for in April 1967, more people than ever joined marches in New York and San Francisco. Estimates of the New York march ran from 100,000 to 250,000 people, and that of San Francisco around 70,000. Spurred on by the progress made since the early marches, the young radicals made the summer of 1967 into a time for combined onslaught against the "war-making machinery of government." Thousands of centers were set up to distribute antiwar information, and Americans were asked to write their congressmen and demand an end to the war.

All of this preparation and work was leading to the most spectacular of all the marches, the March on the Pentagon of October 17, 1967. The antiwar movement hoped to create a massive outpouring of feeling against the war and concentrate this feeling for a few days in Washington, where it could be seen by generals, the president, and congress.

When the March on the Pentagon took place, it was successful beyond the dreams and hopes of most of its organizers. The complete range of the left was there, from the members of the "Lincoln Brigade"—the Americans who had fought fascism in Spain during the thirties—to student Maoist groups. Liberal Democrats joined the march, as did Peace Corps veterans, pacifist groups, and World War II veterans against the war. The Women's Strike for Peace, groups of young people attached to Old Left organizations such as Progressive Labor, hippies, and others swelled the ranks. Some waved American flags; others hoisted Vietcong flags. Well over 100,000 people gathered around the Reflecting Pool between the Washington Monument and the Lincoln Memorial to march to Arlington where, in the Pentagon, the world's largest building, military leaders were planning expansion of the war. Among the speakers who addressed the rally was Dr. Benjamin Spock, the famous pediatrician who had provided the child-rearing theories by which many of the children of the New Left were brought up. Dr. Spock had supported Lyndon Johnson in 1964, but had grown increasingly radical as the war in Vietnam expanded. By 1967 he had become one of the most influential older leaders of the new radicalism.

Most of the demonstrators listened to the speakers addressing the rally and then marched to the Pentagon with no more intent than to make themselves seen, and leave. Others, however, had come to Washington to do more than "vote with their feet." They wanted to create an unforgettable confrontation with the city and federal government, something that would go down in history as more than just another march. These radicals marched to the Pentagon with the others, but remained at the building. They did not get on buses or into cars for the trip back home. Through the evening and night they besieged the Pentagon hoping to break through the troops and marshals guarding it. They stuck flowers into the rifles of the soldiers and asked them to join the antiwar cause. They sang songs such as "The Battle Hymn of the Republic" and "We Shall Overcome." A group of hippies performed the religious rite of exorcism on the Pentagon to cleanse it of devils and evil spirits.

As the night wore on, tempers wore short and more violent confrontation became inevitable. The more extreme demonstrators wanted the troops and marshals to react violently and club them, so that the nation would hear of brutality. Federal marshals were angered by the radicals and were taunted by challenges and obscenities. In the final skirmishes many demonstrators were beaten and arrested and taken to makeshift prisons outside of Washington. Among them was Norman Mailer, whose book *The Armies of the Night* is a lively and moving description of the march and its significance.

More marches were held in 1968; in November 1969 the largest demonstrations in the history of the antiwar movement took place in Washington. Soon, however, this form of activity began to disappear. When the United States invaded Cambodia in the late spring of 1970, most radicals chose more violent methods of protest; they burned campus ROTC buildings or talked of joining underground terrorist groups. Marching was no longer enough.

The people participating in teach-ins and demonstrations had been expressing two types of antiwar sentiment. The first was moderate and democratic, and sometimes morally inspired. It thought that America had done wrong to enter the war, and that a change of course was needed. This sentiment did not believe that America was a moral monster, but simply thought that the nation had blundered. Some New Left members agreed with this position and felt that speaking out against the war would bring Congress around to the antiwar position.

But a second, smaller, and more deeply committed number of people believed that teach-ins and demonstrations accomplished nothing. These people wanted to confront the system with violence and vent their rage physically. The majority of the New Left moved to this position. They were the ones who shouted down opposition at the teach-ins and joined in the attack on the Pentagon. Some were self-righteous new leftists who thought their cause justified any tactic; others were full of genuine despair that the government had not listened to their earlier pleas, but instead had expanded the war.

These radicals found other means of opposing the war. As early as the spring of 1965, a few young men had burned their draft cards as a means of announcing their refusal to go to Southeast Asia. Congress had made it unlawful to destroy the cards, ordering that a heavy fine be imposed for this act along with a possible prison sentence. But this did not deter the occurrence of the act; by the time of the March on the Pentagon, thousands of draft-age students had put a match to their cards, and a few had gone to prison. Some young men, the estimates ranged from 40,000 to 80,000 by 1971, found draft-card burning inadequate and left the country for Canada and elsewhere to avoid the draft.

Those already in the army also began to protest. Coffee houses were established near large bases to distribute information and act as centers where antiwar GI's could assemble. Some soldiers stationed in Europe escaped, aided by an underground of European New Left groups, to Sweden. Captain Howard Levy, stationed at Fort Jackson in South Carolina, refused to give medical instruction to special forces being sent to Vietnam, saying that he could not in good conscience use his medical knowledge to train men who would bomb and kill innocent people. He was sentenced to hard labor for his disobedience.

These deeds angered middle-class America perhaps more than any other activity of the New Left, for the young men who refused to go to war were considered cowards. Most Americans refused to see the courage it took for a young man to stand up for his beliefs and go against the laws of the country and the demands of society. Many young men found themselves terribly alone in prison, or in Canada or Sweden as a result of acting according to their principles. The decision to leave or desert was not an easy one.

Radicals found yet other means of expression. Draft boards across the country were broken into and damaged or destroyed. In Catonsville, Maryland, nine radical Catholics made a fire of the local draft files and records. They were protesting a system, they said, that sent young Americans to kill and die in Southeast Asia. Two priests, who took part in the Catonsville action, emerged as leaders of the Catholic radicals. The Reverends Philip and Daniel Berrigan are brothers who combine Christianity with left-wing political commitment. They argue that a Christian cannot stand apart from the moral and social problems of his time and must enter the struggle on the side he feels to be right. Following this idea, the Berrigans became two of the most famous and committed of New Left radicals, spending much time in hiding from the FBI or in prison. Philip Berrigan and several others became nationally known when they were accused, and later acquitted, of plotting to kidnap Henry Kissinger, adviser to President Nixon.

Many in the New Left began speaking of ways "to bring the war home." They argued that Vietnam was too remote from America and that people were lulled into a false sense of security because of the distance. If American society itself were disrupted and challenged, they said, then the horror and evil of Vietnam would be clear to thousands who rarely thought about it.

Those who wanted "to bring the war home" disrupted trains and boats that carried supplies destined for Vietnam. In the San Francisco Bay Area, young people lay down in front of diesel trains and trucks; in the New York area, they paddled in canoes and small boats out to ships to block passage out of the harbor. The New Left was now—1968—at the height of its power and activity. Dues-paying members of SDS numbered 6,000, but they could rely on many more, 70,000 to 100,000, to join readily in their activities. Many more thousands of students, estimates run as high as 700,000 out of a total student population in the United States of 7,000,000, were sympathetic to New Left and SDS aims and goals. Nor was SDS the only important New Left organization; The National Conference for New Politics (NCNP) and the Peace and Freedom Party (PFP) likewise struggled for peace and revolutionary social change.

But still the war did not end. Frustration and despair deepened, and radicalism grew. New leftists began to dispute among themselves about tactics and strategy. SDS itself began to split and divide into factions advocating varying degrees of radicalism.

Leftist political movements, historically, have always fallen into factionalism and bitter division. Lenin, the leader of the Russian Revolution knew this and demanded that his followers give absolute loyalty to his policy. He did not want them bickering among themselves, for this would weaken their cause and give strength to the enemy. The New Left, however, had no Lenin to lead them, and had little knowledge of history to guide them. Even a rudimentary knowledge of past revolutions would have shown them where they were heading.

The split in SDS was created by a dispute over who would lead and control the organization. A group of Old Left oriented students called Progressive Labor (PL) wanted to establish close contact with the American working class and have student revolutionary work guided solely by the needs of revolutionary workers, a group which existed only in the minds of young radicals. Another faction wanted to maintain SDS as a revolutionary student movement, free to act on its own. PL demanded that SDS act only when commanded by the working class; the other faction wanted to continue antiwar activity independently. After several months of bitter dispute in 1969 and 1970, PL won nominal control of the organization, and SDS split into several distinct factions with no connection to the original group.

The most important and radical of these factions was the Weatherman, which took its name from a song written by Bob Dylan. The Weathermen believed that the only way to bring revolution to America was to continue the struggle against the war machine of the government, and to bring that struggle to a level of total war. They thought that by armed struggle against America they would raise the "revolutionary consciousness" of the workers and the poor and would bring them into the revolution. The Weathermen wanted alliance with the Black Panthers, whom they thought to be the most advanced revolutionaries in America.

The Weathermen were thus the first American terrorist organization, since the days of John Brown. Their magazine, at first called *New Left Notes,* was changed to the threatening *Fire,* referring to *The Fire Next Time,* the title of a book by James Baldwin. Mark Rudd, the leader of the Columbia insurrection, was a Weatherman; another was Bernardine Dohrn who called upon young radicals to take up arms against the powerful and rich. Weathermen referred to America as "Amerika," the German spelling with a "k" implying a Nazi German-type tyrannical and fascist state. They established collectives in Michigan and Ohio during the summer of 1969 to train students in guerrilla tactics, bomb making, and street fighting. By the fall of 1969, they thought they were ready to put their training into action.

A series of violent confrontations with police occurred in Chicago in September and October, culminating in the "Days of Rage" between October 8 and 11. Helmeted Weathermen charged down busy Chicago streets breaking windows and frightening onlookers. To the revolutionaries it seemed as though they were bringing America to its knees; to onlookers it seemed more like a small number of young people were acting out revolutionary fantasies. Several

Weathermen leaders were arrested for assault, property damage, and other felonies.

In the following month, Weathermen tried to charge the Vietnamese embassy in Washington, only to be repelled by police. They then ran down Massachusetts Avenue, damaging police vans and cars. On Connecticut Avenue, they threw rocks through store windows. Later, they besieged the Department of Justice (calling it the Department of Injustice), again breaking windows. They took down an American flag and hoisted a Vietcong flag in its place.

Further bombings and incidents that followed were attributed to Weathermen activity. On March 6, 1970, on a fashionable street in Manhattan's Greenwich Village, a townhouse exploded and was utterly destroyed. Investigation showed that Weathermen, including the daughter of the wealthy owner of the house, had been using the basement for making bombs and that at least three young radicals had been killed in the blast. The daughter, who survived, went into and remains in hiding. On June 9, a New York police station was bombed, and on July 23, thirteen Weathermen were indicted for planning a whole series of such attacks on police stations. The first of many bombings of the Bank of America on July 27 was likewise claimed by the Weathermen.

Violence mounted on the other side too. In May 1970, at the height of student demonstrations against the invasion of Cambodia, four students were killed and several wounded when the National Guard fired upon a student group at Kent State University in Ohio. The university had been the scene of disruption and violence for several days. Its ROTC building had been burned, and the town threatened by angry radicals. The governor sent the guard to restore order, but the young, inexperienced soldiers were thrown into panic by the rock-throwing students. A volley of shots was fired and the wounded students, including some bystanders, fell to the ground. At first, the demonstrators failed to comprehend what had happened, for many had been told that the guard would not use real ammunition. A nationwide reaction of concern followed this incident.

Other bombings took place at the University of Wisconsin where a math and physics building was damaged, and a

lions of Americans were so fed up with the system that they would welcome the chance to become revolutionaries?

The answer, I believe, for the absurdity of Weatherman policy, lies in the degree to which the Weathermen were acting out generational revolt, and merely assuming revolutionary roles as a way of shocking and frightening the older generation. Weathermen were not true revolutionaries in the sense of Lenin or Mao Tse-tung. They did not take stock of their situation and of their own relative weakness, and then coordinate their activities. True revolutionaries know that they must not destroy their movement by overcommitment or spreading themselves too thinly. The Weathermen did just the opposite: they deliberately sought to overcommit themselves; they deliberately sought confrontation with the overwhelming power of the government even though they knew their numbers to be insignificant.

This decision, it seems likely, originated deep in the personalities of Weathermen, in a need to revolt totally against the older generation, perhaps even the need to destroy themselves. They played the part of Mao, Castro, or Lenin in order to shock their parents and find a sense of identity of their own. Had they really been Mao, Castro, or Lenin, however, they would not so readily have sought confrontation and martyrdom.

It is interesting to note that successful revolutions, the Russian, the Chinese, and the Cuban, have carefully put an end to extremism; a clamp is put on those who would carry the movement beyond certain limits. Lenin's treatise on *Left-wing Communism: An Infantile Disorder* (1920) condemned those who were "enchanted" by a certain kind of working-class revolution, but who were not willing to examine the one-sidedness of their thinking. He asked the radicals to see reality and not carry revolution beyond the stage that society was prepared for. Finally, in his attack on revolutionary extremists, Lenin quoted Engels, the friend and associate of Marx, who said, "What childish innocence it is to present impatience as a theoretically convincing argument!" The Weathermen and other New Left extremists who demanded a "Revolution, Now!" had no platform but their impatience.

Mao had another means of confronting radicals who

wanted to carry the revolution further than circumstances would permit. In 1968, when he saw that the youth movement, the Red Guards, were carrying their "purification" of Chinese society to uncalled-for lengths, he sent them to the countryside. Large numbers of students worked in the rice paddies and helped with harvests throughout China. It was Mao's belief that hard work would reform the radicals and bring them back to reality.

Another characteristic of the New Left was carried to extreme during the second phase of development. This quality was the "know-nothing" attitude of many young radicals who cared nothing for the past or history, and who thought they could help society start anew with no reference to the past. This attitude was derived in part from the self-righteousness we have seen at work in the movement. When people believe they have some special reform to make in society, they begin to think that their work is completely new and free of the mistakes of the past; they forget that everything that exists is rooted in history.

The loss of a sense of reality in the later New Left can be attributed to a loss of touch with the past. The civil rights movement of the early phase succeeded in large part because it raised questions that touched traditions long a part of American history—equality, justice for all, and fair play. The terrorism of the Weathermen or Samuel Melville, however, was not rooted in the American past, and for that reason alone the Weathermen and Melville found themselves talking to no one.

The New Left in America was not alone in its course from moderation to extreme radicalism. The young radical movements of Japan, Germany, and France followed a similar pattern, with some variations. The next chapter will trace the evolution of the New Left in these other affluent countries.

# 5 THE NEW LEFT ABROAD: JAPAN, FRANCE, AND GERMANY

## JAPAN

The earliest, largest, and most dramatic of youth movements in recent years has been the Japanese. Pictures of helmeted students battling Tokyo police became a familiar sight in the newspapers of the late 1950s. Indeed, when three young Japanese radicals slaughtered more than twenty people at Tel Aviv Airport in the early seventies, the world was shocked, but not overly surprised. The deep commitment of Japanese leftists and their willingness to die for their beliefs were well known.

The three terrorists in the Tel Aviv incident were acting in support of Palestinian liberation. They had made the Arab cause against Israel their own because they saw the Arabs as victims of aggression and exploitation. The young Japanese students were deeply anti-American and identified, as New Left students the world over, with the downtrodden and revolutionary peoples of the Third World.

The Japanese students were likewise acting in a tradition of student radicalism that went back to the years immediately following World War II. At that time, young people were profoundly critical of the older generation, which had brought years of warfare and defeat upon the nation. They were determined to root out of power all those people connected with the former government. They demanded that teachers and educators who had been connected with the military regime be dismissed; they wanted changes in universities to bring them up to modern, democratic standards. Leftist students began organizing into groups that would fight to keep Japan democratic and prevent the return of the old order.

The most dynamic of the student groups to be founded after the war was the Zengakuren, whose name is formed from a Japanese phrase meaning "All Japan Federation of College Student Governments." The Zengakuren was established on September 18, 1948, by the Communist party of Japan. Its charter described the purpose of the group as the "security and improvement of student life." But the Zengakuren was also to seek "equal opportunities for education" for all and defend academic freedom; any encroachment by the Japanese government on the rights of teachers or students was to be attacked and condemned. The charter went further and said students should work to "defend peace and democracy" in the country as a whole. The Zengakuren adopted the slogan, "Peace, Democracy, and the Betterment of Student Life." The students had not only entrusted the care of the universities to themselves, they had likewise volunteered to watch over the nation and see that it did not slide into tyranny and militarism.

The Zengakuren addressed itself immediately to the problem of university reform. A few months before the Zengakuren's organization, 200,000 Japanese students had struck throughout the country against the raising of university fees. The fees had been raised anyway, and the Zengakuren utilized the resentment caused by the government's seeming lack of concern for students. A protest began at Kyoto University, where two hundred students occupied the office of the president, and kept him prisoner. It took three hundred police to free him, while the strike continued at Kyoto for a month and a half.

Anti-Americanism gave the movement impetus. An American professor attempted to make a tour of Japan asking for the ouster of communist teachers; to the Zengakuren, he seemed to be arguing for the restoration of the old order and the return of the fascist professors. When he spoke, students disrupted his speeches. Attacks were made on American soldiers stationed in Japan; when the Korean War broke out and more American troops began landing in Japan, police had to raid Zengakuren headquarters to insure the safety of Americans. The Americans at the head of the occupation government found it necessary to forbid student strikes and demonstrations.

After the Korean War, student activity quieted for a while, only to flare up again in May 1956. Students protested the testing of hydrogen bombs by the United States and accused the Japanese government of returning to the wartime tyranny and suppression of free speech. Between 1956 and 1958, a severe break developed between the Zengakuren and the leaders of the Communist party, which had sponsored Zengakuren activity. The old leftists accused the young radicals of being "Trotskyite," that is, of refusing to follow party instructions and of pursuing an individual course of action. The leaders of the Zengakuren were kicked out of the Communist party and told that their undisciplined and spontaneous radical activism had nothing to do with the cause of world communism.

In the next two years, on its own, the Zengakuren reached the peak of its activity and influence. Estimates vary on the membership at that time, but figures usually range between three and four hundred thousand out of a total student population of 709,000. By the end of 1960, the students brought about the fall of one government and had caused an American president, Dwight Eisenhower, to cancel a state visit to Japan on the occasion of the renewal of the Japanese-American Mutual Security Treaty.

Even before its break with the Communist party, the Zengakuren had revealed the New Left slant of its philosophy. It had characteristically relied more on instinctive and spontaneous reaction to problems than on theory and discussion. It reacted to specific problems, such as university reform, hydrogen bomb testing, or the Korean War, and dealt with them immediately, learning in the process of acting. Rather than discussing the society they sought to create, the Japanese New Left chose action and seemed to believe that action, if it were guided by idealism, would lead to better conditions.

Other characteristics of the Zengakuren likewise proved a pattern of the later New Left movement in America and elsewhere. Japanese radicals tried to ally themselves with the working class, only to meet rejection. The Zengakuren supported striking mine workers at the Miike Mines and thought they would establish a union of student and worker radicalism. The miners, however, asked the students to leave; they wanted nothing to do with the young radicals who acted too often without thinking and upset the delicate negotiations between the miners and the mine owners.

The student radicals of Japan showed the same absolutism and puritanism about their cause that the American New Left was later to display. The older generation was totally corrupt and could not be trusted. Only the youth movement preserved purity of cause and principle, only it could save society. It is likewise interesting to note that the members of the Zengakuren came from the middle- and upper middle-income families in Japan. Members of other classes could rarely afford to go to the universities and did not have the time or energy to devote to politics.

After the height of its activity in 1960, the Zengakuren quickly fell into division and factionalism. Members disputed with one another on the nature of the organization and its goals. The different factions that emerged are confusing and need not be elaborated. Since the radicals could not agree on what to do or define who the enemy was, the vigor and power of student politics declined. Students continued to make their voices heard from time to time, but the huge demonstrations of the fifties and 1960 were no longer seen. A meeting held in 1962 to commemorate a girl student, Michiko Kamba, who had died in the demonstration of

1960, ended in a free-for-all as leftist students viciously attacked one another.

Some armed violence on the part of students took place at Waseda University in 1964. Waseda is a leading private institution in Japan, and, as a private institution, often finds it difficult to acquire adequate funds. Student fees were high and threatened to go higher. The university expanded enrollment to collect more student fees, but did not have facilities to take care of the new students. The radicals at Waseda were protesting student costs and overcrowding; they were likewise attacking the remoteness and lack of sensitivity to student needs on the part of the administration.

Japanese leftists continued to be active in anti-American protest during the sixties. They roundly condemned the Vietnam War, and several student groups attempted to stop American war supplies and troop movement. Japanese radicals offered aid to American war protesters and helped young soldiers and sailors who did not want to serve in Southeast Asia to escape the army and navy. But in spite of this activity, the New Left has declined, and some observers believe that it will come to an end. Other commentators prefer to wait, for they remind us that the Japanese radicals may be having a period of quiet, like the one between 1952 and 1956. The massacre at Tel Aviv reminds us likewise that Japanese radicals are committed and willing to die for their cause; it is not easy to write off a movement that has such zealous followers.

## FRANCE

The active student left of the sixties in the United States was largely a new creation. America had seen leftist movements before, but had never experienced so large a number of students dedicated to radical politics. In France, and elsewhere in Europe, however, there had been a longer tradition of student activism and of significant leftist protest.

Early in the twentieth century, the National Union of French Students (UNEF) had been formed to coordinate student activity. UNEF had been active between the world wars, but had disappeared during the Nazi occupation of

France. It was revived immediately following the liberation and quickly became an important part of student life.

A postwar statement of purpose was drawn up at Grenoble in 1946 and has come to be known as the "Charter of Grenoble." The charter carefully defined UNEF as a union of workers and paralleled its purpose with that of the trade union movement. Students were called "young intellectual workers" and were told to consider themselves as members of the working class, with no special privileges in society.

The French students saw their duties as two: first, "to define, spread, and defend truth which comprises the duty to propagate and enrich culture and to assess the meaning of history," and, second, "to defend freedom against all oppression." The first duty implied the right of students to judge society and discover better alternatives to existing conditions; the second implied the right of students to act when they found conditions bad.

During the fifties, the students became involved in the cause of Algerian independence, a movement that bore some resemblance to the black liberation movement in the United States. Algeria, in North Africa, had been a colony of France since the nineteenth century. Over the years, Algeria and France had grown close together and had assumed a relationship that was something more than colony and mother country and something less than full assimilation. When France was granting independence to her other possessions she held back with Algeria, planning to maintain its "Frenchness" and keep it as a part of Greater France. Many Frenchmen thought that they were doing a favor for the Algerians, that it would be an honor for the Algerians to have the chance to remain French.

The reality, however, was otherwise. Algerians were second-class people in France and were chosen only for the lower, menial jobs, just as were the blacks in America. Algeria's resources went to France, and little was returned. In Algeria a significant independence movement had arisen, which was put down with great violence by the French army. Algerian freedom fighters and guerrilla warriors were often caught and reportedly tortured; the French were accused of using violence even against innocent Algerians, hoping to frighten the Arabs from support of the independence movement.

French students thus had a cause with which they could identify. They supported the Algerians who fought for separation from France and accused the French government of tyranny, hypocrisy, and inhumanity. Huge demonstrations in support of Algerian freedom were staged by UNEF. France became polarized between those who wanted independence for Algeria and those who were against it. Governments tottered and fell on the issue. Emerging in the early sixties from the Algerian struggle was a highly active and experienced young left, eager for political commitment. When Algeria won her independence, radical students were left for a while suspended without a cause. Basic characteristics of the New Left, however, had been developed. French radicals identified with the Third World and found politics in their own country corrupt and in need of reform.

The issues that came to the front to replace the Algerian question were the educational policies of the government and the authoritarian regime of General Charles de Gaulle. De Gaulle, the hero of World War II, had become head of the French government in the chaos of the Algerian dispute. He granted freedom to Algeria and was perhaps the only man who could unite and quiet the divided country. Through the sixties, however, complaints arose that his government was too bureaucratic, tyrannical, and unconcerned with the common man. Students, of course, were among those most displeased with the general. They had not supported his rise to power; indeed, they had actively dissented from it. The general did not forget this, and his policies toward the university reflected his displeasure. He cut down on subsidies to student-run facilities and established a Gaullist student organization, which he hoped would divide the power of UNEF and weaken student political unity. Students complained that de Gaulle and his government were increasingly insulated from criticism, and that the general held himself aloof from the problems of France. This grievance was one of the chief calls to action during 1968. It was not only the students who felt it; other Frenchmen came to resent the arrogance and power of de Gaulle.

The second rallying point of the sixties was the need for reform of French universities. Between 1945 and 1968, the student population had grown from 123,000 to 514,000. At the Sorbonne alone there were 160,000 students. Dormitories, libraries, lecture halls, laboratories and the other various facilities needed for higher education had not been expanded to match the growth in student population. We saw earlier how the revolution of 1968 began at Nanterre University in a suburb of Paris. Nanterre was one of the new universities built to accommodate thousands of new students, but without adequate building space or facilities.

The students also protested the examination system in France and demanded that it be brought to an end. The examination system is a rigid method of classifying students and their abilities. Often a person's entire future is decided by a score he made on a test he would not be allowed to take again. The *baccalauréat* (called *bac* or *bachot*) determines whether or not a student will be allowed to go to college. The *agrégation* determines whether one can become a secondary school teacher, but is also a test a person has to pass if he desires high office in almost any field in France. College professors must submit to the difficult *doctorat d'état*. These are not the only examinations; many other tests rate students and classify them according to ability or lack of ability. The system is highly undemocratic since rarely can a working-class youth prepare himself for the more difficult exams; he is surpassed by middle-class students who have been trained from childhood to do well on the tests and thus rise in French society.

The unfairness and inflexibility of the examination system were notorious, and French leftist students demanded an end to all testing. The radicals argued that the tests made true education impossible, and that they turned a student's life into a series of confrontations and periods of strain. Radicals likewise called the tests pernicious because they were unfair to the poor and made change impossible in the rigid French society.

In 1962, there were demonstrations protesting overcrowding, and UNEF held student strikes. Some improvement was made, and student opposition declined. UNEF now faced the classic dilemma of leftist groups and began to divide over motives and goals. It attempted to set up "Student Work Groups" to bring the subjects taught in the classroom closer to real, everyday life and to prepare more efficiently for examinations; these groups failed. In March 1966, opposition to a new government educational plan almost destroyed UNEF. UNEF called the new plan "technocratic" and said that it did nothing to alleviate the real grievances of the students. But little student support for UNEF's opposition was forthcoming. Strike meetings were poorly attended; students left for three-day weekends. By 1968, however, the French New Left had reformed and was able to bring off the May Days described in Chapter One.

There are several striking similarities between the French New Left and the American New Left. Both identified early in their histories with an underprivileged, exploited people. In the case of America, it was the black of the South; with the French, the Algerian freedom fighter. Both New Lefts ripened in opposition to a foreign war with an undeveloped nation—Vietnam, and Algeria. Both were concerned deeply with the quality of education and the size of universities. It is interesting to find that French radicals read about the incidents at Berkeley and Columbia and felt much in common with them; indeed, many French radicals thought American radicalism was several years ahead of that of France.

Finally, the French joined the American and Japanese new leftists in condemning American imperialism and in being anti-American. The degree of American hatred in France was high; Daniel Cohn-Bendit, the student leader, argued that nothing that came from America was worth considering, since all was contaminated with exploitation, militarism, and aggression. Anti-American sentiment in France was deeply irrational and intolerant. An American who lived in Paris during the May Days of 1968 and was sympathetic to much that the students demanded recorded that she was at the Sorbonne during one of the endless debates among the radicals. They were discussing what sort of educational system France should have. A system came up that was said to permit students a major and minor subject for several years, followed by years of specialization. The students cheered wildly for the system when they heard it called the "Chinese plan of education." The system was, of course, the American system, but, the belief was, if the students had been presented with a plan called American, they would have booed and hissed it out of the assembly hall. The anti-Americanism reached another peak when the noted philosopher and idol of the New Left, Jean-Paul Sartre, refused to speak at teach-ins in the United States, since he felt that his presence in America might cause the world to believe America was democratic.

The French student movement since 1968 has calmed down and lost its fever pitch. Its success or lack of success is uncertain. Universities seem to have undergone little change, and students are still subjected to examinations. De Gaulle is gone, but his successor has not made any extraordinary changes in government. Terrorism made a brief appearance among the students but was a futile and self-defeating effort. One cannot say that student radicalism has died in France, however, because the French nation has a long history of revolutions (1789, 1830, 1848, and 1871) and students in France are quite aware of that tradition.

## GERMANY

Leftist politics among German students did not begin with the end of World War II as they did in Japan and France. On the contrary, the German student left was as quiet and apathetic as was the American left for many years. There were some few members of the older leftist organizations, but for the most part young people were willing to forego radical political commitment. Perhaps the knowledge of what had happened in Germany in the thirties and forties made them fearful of extremism. Perhaps the uncertainty of Germany's future, divided between East and West, between communism and capitalism, made them politically uninterested and reluctant.

The German New Left was not born until the early sixties. At that time the German Socialist Student Union (SDS, not to be confused with the American SDS; the two are distinct organizations) was expelled from the Social Democratic party for its refusal to abide by the Social Democratic party's rules and regulations. The German SDS had only two hundred members at that time, most of them at the Free University of Berlin.

Work began quickly, however, in several areas. The first was education. German universities had experienced the same enormous expansion that French universities had, and like the French, had not done enough to prepare for it. Facilities were inadequate; classrooms were overcrowded. Also, German universities were even less democratic than French; fewer students had an opportunity for higher education, and only 5 percent of all German university students came from the working class. In the face of these problems, the German New Left drew up a plan for university reform that is considered by many to be excellent and quite useful.

Beyond education, the New Left concerned itself with the German past and strove to atone for the murder of millions of Jews and others during World War II. An exhibition about the Nazi treatment of the Jew was put together and shown in several cities. In fact, the German New Left has come to identify with the Jew in much the same way that American radicals identified with the black. Rudi Dutschke, the leader of the German New Left, called his followers "today's Jews" and warned them that they must avoid tyranny and prevent the return of a new Hitler. In much the same way, German radical identification with the Third World has been easy. It is interesting that many German radicals participated in the civil rights movement in the American South. They suffered along with the American New Left, and some spent time in jails in Mississippi, taking back to Germany with them valuable experience in political and social reform.

In noticeable distinction from the New Left movements in other countries, however, the New Left in Germany has from its conception striven to be "scientific," and more traditionally Marxist. This does not mean that it denies the value of spontaneity and immediate action as stressed in Japan, France, or the United States. Rather it has meant that more planning and theory are discussed than elsewhere, and more emphasis is placed on learning from experience everything that experience has to offer. The German New

Left likewise seems more willing to learn from the past than other New Left movements.

By the spring of 1965, the German New Left was becoming quite active and committed to protest. An occasion that marked the change in its activity was a celebration of the twentieth anniversary of liberation from fascism scheduled by the Free University. Karl Jaspers, a prominent German philosopher, was asked to speak, but could not because of ill health. Students asked that Erich Kuby, a radical journalist, be chosen to replace Jaspers. Kuby had made himself unwelcome to the university by his repeated attacks on it. Kuby felt the Free University was a political tool since it had been established in West Berlin as a counterpart to the Marxist university of East Berlin. For Kuby, the Free University was nothing but a political arm of West German democracy and capitalism. The university rejected the student request for Kuby and dismissed a young professor who spoke on behalf of the students.

The student body became highly incensed; demonstrations and strikes followed. SDS accused the university of remoteness and lack of concern for students. They demanded that the administration be changed in order to give students more voice in university affairs.

The protest over the university's denial of free speech quickly flared into a protest over the Vietnam War and the invasion of the Dominican Republic by American troops. The students demanded the resignation of the rector of the university, as well as the ouster of the United States from Southeast Asia and the Caribbean. The fight reached its most bitter phase in May and June of 1965. Out of a student body of 6,000, some 4 percent, or 250 students (compare this with the 5 percent of the student body at Berkeley who could be called "hard-core radicals"), manned barricades at the university. A new, more liberal rector was appointed for the next term, but other student demands were only partially met. Furthermore, the university moved to prohibit all political activity in the future.

The question the new radicals had raised for Germany was a difficult one. SDS had announced that its radicalism would challenge society and thereby help preserve democracy in Germany. But to many people, the activities of 1965 seemed too much like the activity of the Nazi Youth in the early thirties. Indeed, many Germans referred to the New Left as "leftist fascism." Nazi Youth had concentrated on the universities and had demanded that the educational system be changed to fit their notion of what Germany should be. Nazi Youth had gone a long way toward helping Hitler to power, and in the process had destroyed the universities. Germans feared that the extremism of the New Left would likewise lead to a situation where the universities would be harmed rather than helped. The reason, therefore, that the administration sought to end politics on campus was rooted in the fear that the Nazi past could be repeated.

There was a second reason for the caution of the Free University in dealing with the radicals. The Free University wanted to remain an institution where a variety of opinions could be heard and taught. The universities of East Germany taught only one political and philosophical system— that of Marxism-Leninism. There was thus some fear that leftist students, in their zeal for educational reform and improvement, would turn the university into a school along Marxist lines.

The university's prohibition of political activity, of course, did nothing to stem the tide of student radicalism. SDS grew to 2,500 members by 1967 and had organizations at many West German universities. A general SDS policy of "provocation" was developed that sought to keep democratic issues before the people of the country and prevent relapse into authoritarianism. "Provocations" were not necessarily to be violent, but they were to be dramatic enough to remind the public that alternatives existed to government policy.

A state visit by the Shah of Iran provided the stimulus for such a series of provocative acts. The shah was a symbol, to the students, of old-style exploitative government. They saw him as an extremely rich man who had done nothing beneficial for his people. The shah was likewise a close friend of the United States, and was viewed as one of those tyrants kept in office by American money and military aid. Radicals throughout Germany demonstrated against him wherever he appeared. The largest protest occurred in Berlin. Students had demonstrated for hours, but when the shah went to the State Opera, the police turned on the young people. Many were severely beaten. One demonstrator, Benno Ohnesorg, was shot in the back of the head by a plain-clothes policeman. He was a young Protestant who had no deep political commitment.

On June 8, 1967, the day of his funeral, lecture halls across Germany were empty. A vast strike was held. Germany was shaken by the death, and the chief of the Berlin police was forced to resign. Ohnesorg's death was followed during the Easter vacation of 1968 with an assassination attempt on Rudi Dutschke, the leader of West Germany's New Left. "Red Rudi," as he was dubbed by the German press, was seriously wounded by a right-wing house painter. German students argued that the attack on Dutschke had been spurred on by editorials in the newspapers and magazines connected with the Axel Springer publishing firm. Radicals attacked buildings owned by Springer and demanded an end to the "fascist press."

The New Left continues to be active in Germany. The Free University is still divided, and many important professors have left the institution. A thirty-three-year-old rector is now in charge. In 1969, students were given the right to vote on such matters as teaching evaluation, research, and the distribution of university funds.

The German New Left has grown since 1968, and many student radicals are committed to total change of German society. A deep anti-Americanism encouraged by the Vietnam War and by the continued American presence in Germany has become central to the movement. Recently, one of the most popular soccer stars of Germany, Paul Breitner, announced his conversion to radicalism and had his picture taken beside his posters of Che Guevara and Mao Tsetung. A small group of ultra-left young people dedicated to violence and terrorism has appeared. In 1972, a number of these activists—they called themselves anarchists—were arrested in connection with the bombing of American army bases. Finally, it should be said that the German New Left, just like the New Left of France, America, and Japan, is overwhelmingly middle class in make-up. German radicals come from affluent, professional homes as do American radicals.

. . .

Similar radical movements exist in other developed, affluent countries. Holland had its *Studenten Vakbeweging,* an organization that has combined protest for better student conditions with protest against the Vietnam War. Holland likewise has its "Provos"—young men and women who are committed to disrupting the settled bourgeois life of their country, and who greatly resemble the beatniks and hippies of America, but add a more dynamic, active lifestyle to their bohemianism. "Provos"—the name is taken from provocateurs—believe in nothing but their own exuberance. They demand feeling, love, and experience. They are unorganized, but are nevertheless threatening to the average Dutchman, who sees them as lazy, unwashed, and crazy.

England has a small, but active New Left which has not indulged in violence or extremism, but which nevertheless has published newspapers, organized demonstrations, and protested conditions at several universities, including Leeds and the London School of Economics. It was, after all, the young radicals of England who evolved the peace symbol now known the world over, the circle with the diameter cut up through the middle and two radii, like halffolded wings on the sides (the symbol was derived from the semaphore signals for "N" and "D"—Nuclear Disarmament). In Italy, a New Left movement has rioted and struck at the universities in Turin, Rome, and Milan and has been blamed for acts of terrorism that killed innocent bystanders in 1969.

The New Left movements of the sixties have several things in common. Each has concentrated on university reform, followed by broader political commitment that includes anti-Americanism and attacks on bureaucracy and bigness in government. Tactics and issues have varied somewhat from country to country, but basic concerns have been the same. There was no international organization coordinating student revolt around the world, but there were problems that crossed national borders and that were shared by all industrialized, affluent countries. It was these shared problems that the various New Lefts attacked, and it is not surprising that they came up with similar solutions, or that they looked to one another for advice and ideas.

The common problems that the New Left shared, however, were not the problems attacked by other revolutionary movements in the world. The youth of Czechoslovakia or Poland who demonstrated in 1968 were fighting for basic freedoms long enjoyed in the affluent countries—freedom of speech, freedom of assembly, the so-called bourgeois freedoms. They shared little with the demands of the New Left. When radical Czech and West German students met in Berlin in 1967, the two groups found themselves puzzled by one another. The West Germans spoke of their desire for economic control and socialist planning; the Czechs spoke of their need for the bourgeois freedoms. The conference ended in a stalemate when the delegations discovered they could not reach a common understanding of specific revolutionary goals.

Likewise, the revolutionary movements of the Third World —in Uruguay, Turkey, Mozambique, and elsewhere—were distant from the young radicals of America, Japan, or Europe. New leftists identified with the Third World revolutionaries, but the Third World revolutionaries, who were fighting for food, shelter, and basic human needs, found little in common with the New Left. The New Left was only one of several types of revolution that have manifested themselves in the modern world.

# 6 YOUNG REVOLUTIONARIES OF THE PAST

The rebellion of the young illustrates again that there is nothing new under the sun. Most civilizations, from those of Ancient Egypt and Sumer, to the small isolated cultures of South Sea Islands, have recorded conflicts between fathers and sons, between generation and generation. Students at the Sorbonne in the thirteenth century rioted over the quality of their food and wine. There was a German student movement in the early nineteenth century that aspired to unite Germany and was highly nationalistic. The young German radicals wore beards, the first example in history of the beard as a revolutionary symbol, and accused their elders of being corrupt and weak. Students also played decisive roles in the radical movements of Burma in the 1930s, in Korea after 1919, and in China from 1903 to the present.

Many of the most notable and successful revolutionaries have been young men. Jefferson was thirty-two in 1775, at the beginning of the American Revolution. Madison was twenty-four, Alexander Hamilton was twenty, and the Marquis de Lafayette, eighteen. Among the significant French revolutionaries, Robespierre was only thirty-six when put to the guillotine; the flamboyant St. Just, twenty-seven. Napoleon was twenty-eight when he made a name for himself as the most brilliant general of the French Republican Army. Castro and Che were in their twenties when they led the Cuban Revolution. A young man of eighteen, Gavrilo Princip, precipitated World War I by joining with fellow radicals in Bosnia (present-day Yugoslavia) and assassinating the heir to the Austrian throne. Ho Chi Minh was a young student in Paris when he became radicalized. It should not surprise anyone that the energy of youth often manifests itself in political activity and social reform.

The two revolutionary movements that have been most often compared to the New Left are the Russian student movement of the last half of the nineteenth century and the Nazi student movement in Germany in the twenties and thirties of this century. Both critics and admirers of the New Left have pointed out its similarity to the Russian movement; only the critics, of course, have claimed that the New Left resembled the Nazi Youth organization. We shall look at both the Russian and German movements in order to draw our own conclusions.

Russia in the nineteenth century was a vast country ruled by a czar and a small noble class. Together, the czar and nobility owned most of the land and wealth, while the peasant class—over 90 percent of the population—remained poor, ignorant, and superstitious. Up to 1861, the peasants were held in a form of slavery known as serfdom, which required that they work the land for their lords and made it impossible for them to own their own land. Liberation did little to improve their condition. Often the land they were given was small and poor and would not sustain a family. They had to sell to the lord or work for him at low wages.

Reform and change were made impossible by an intolerant czar and a ruling class that feared anything new and different that might challenge their favored position. A secret police force was established to investigate students and others who might bring new ideas from western Europe into Russia. One czar forbade the importation of sheet music from France and Germany for fear that it might be revolutionary tracts written in code.

It is not surprising that, in spite of these restrictions, a revolutionary movement began to appear among young men and women who knew that conditions were better outside of Russia and who realized that things might be changed. In late 1825, a group of young army officers were arrested for planning a revolt against the czar. The young men had some vague notion of revolution followed by liberal reform and the redistribution of wealth and land. "The Decembrists," as they came to be known, were quickly dispersed and their leaders executed, but the story of their effort spread across the country and stirred the imaginations of many.

Czar Nicholas I (1825–55), who had just taken office when the Decembrists were discovered, moved to destroy any further radicalism. He expanded the secret police and appointed men to his cabinet who were ultraconservative. The revolutionaries were effectively silenced for a while. Significant student activity did not arise again until 1857 and 1858 when young people at the universities of Moscow and Kharkov protested police surveillance of their activities.

By 1861 the student movement had become full-blown. Forty-three percent of the student body of St. Petersburg (today called Leningrad) University were imprisoned, and the university was closed for two years. The initial provocation had been the refusal by the university to allow a professor to make a speech, but broader political problems were in the air, particularly the liberation of the serfs. Uprisings followed at university towns across Russia. At Moscow several students were killed by police and cossacks. Kazan and Kharkov likewise rebelled and were suppressed.

The student movements did not limit themselves to demands for university reform and freedom. Very early, radical students formed secret groups that discussed the social and economic problems of Russia and advocated radical and revolutionary reform. At Kazan, twenty young men formed the "Society of Communists." A manifesto called "Young Russia" was secretly printed and distributed; it presented the radical views of many Russian young men and women.

The young of Russia were adopting progressive ideas borrowed from France, Germany, and England. They were ashamed that Russia was backward and ignorant. Above all, they were attracted to the scientific developments of the West and found in science a means of confronting the mysticism and superstition of the offical Russian Orthodox Church. Science taught them to accept as true only the things they could see and examine objectively. The young men and women who were so strongly influenced by science that they rejected religion and Russian backwardness were called nihilists. Nihilism implied that they believed in nothing, but this was not quite true. They did believe in the scientific method of thinking and believed that it should be applied to all realms of life—to religion, government, and society as well as to nature. The nihilists were immortalized in the greatest of all novels about generational conflict, *Fathers and Sons,* by Ivan Turgenev.

By 1870, the student movement had begun the most inspired and prodigious undertaking of its history, its movement "to the people." Older Russian revolutionaries long in exile in England and France had urged that the young, dedicated people of Russia go to the peasants of the countryside and convert them to the revolutionary creed. The new radical young needed no deep prodding to respond; the idea caught on, and between 1870 and 1875 thousands of students from the metropolitan centers of the country went into the backward areas of Russia. The movement came to be known in Russia as the *narodniki* movement, *narodniki* coming from the word for people. The movement might also be called a Populist movement.

One of the young revolutionaries who worked in the countryside has described the feeling of the movement in these words:

*Nothing had ever been seen that was anything like it. It was revelation rather than propaganda. . . . It was a powerful cry that came from no one knows where and called people to redeem Russia and humanity. When they heard the cry, people rose with sadness and unhappiness for the past. They gave up homes, riches, honor, and family. They joined the cause with joy, enthusiasm, and faith which a person feels only once, and if once lost, cannot be revived. . . . It was not a political movement as of yet. It was rather more like a religious movement. Men were not just being practical . . . but they wanted to satisfy a duty they felt and a need for moral perfection.*

With no revision, these words could have been spoken about early New Left activity in the American South.

Russian students shed their uniforms and put on the garb of the peasants. They chose to live simple lives in simple surroundings. They ate the food of the peasant and drank his vodka. The student who wrote the words previously quoted became a stonecutter in Tver; others worked as teachers. One became a "vaccinator" and helped immunize the peasants against smallpox. The students exposed the injustices of the taxation system and the laws of land tenure. They distributed pamphlets about the great peasant revolts of past centuries and hoped thereby that the peasant would realize his poor situation and revolt against the government.

Only in one instance did the *narodniki* succeed in bringing about a peasant uprising, and that was in Chigirin in 1877. The young radicals told the peasants that the czar wanted them to revolt against the nobility, and only then did the peasants fight. Otherwise, the movement to the people was a dismal failure. Peasants the world over are a conservative lot, and usually deeply religious. In this case, they resented the lack of Christian faith among the students and did not approve of the student's dressing in peasant costume. Often the peasants beat up the students, or got them drunk with vodka, and ran them out of the village.

In the face of the overwhelming defeat of their idealism, many students turned to acts of terrorism and violence against the government and police. Even before the failure of the *narodniki* movement, terrorism had developed as an alternative to moderation; to some it appeared the only course open for those who wanted to change Russia. The most sinister of the early terrorist groups was founded by

Sergei Nechaev (pronounced Ne-cheye-iff). Nechaev, the son of a serf, had educated himself and had then become a teacher in a seminary. At nineteen he was already organizing his acquaintances into groups of revolutionaries committed and dedicated to nothing but the revolution. With his extraordinary personality, Nechaev convinced his friends that he was head of a vast underground revolutionary movement which could rise up and overthrow the czar. The organization existed only in his imagination, but not only did he convince his associates of its existence, but he was likewise able to persuade the Russian anarchist, Michael Bakunin, who was living in exile in Switzerland, that the secret group was a reality. Bakunin admired the energy and dedication of Nechaev and arranged for him to get money from other Russian exiles to finance the cause of revolution.

Nechaev organized several of his immediate friends into cells or groups of four. There was great secrecy in the organization, and the members knew nothing of what their plans were, displaying absolute loyalty and trust to Nechaev. When one of his young student followers dared to question his orders, Nechaev shot him in the head. The police discovered the group and arrested them, but their leader had escaped to Switzerland. Later, Russian police seized Nechaev there and returned him to Russia for trial.

At the trial, a book written in code was read before the public. It was Nechaev's secret book on revolution, entitled *Catechism of a Revolutionary*. The catechism horrified many of the young revolutionaries who were as yet moderates; but Nechaev's catechism was prophetic, for its belief became the belief of many young Russians who were to be frustrated after the failure of the "to the people" movement.

The first paragraph of the revolutionary catechism is the most blatant statement in history of what it means to be a revolutionary:

*The revolutionary is a lost man; he has no interests of his own . . . no feelings, no habits, no belongings . . . everything in him is absorbed by a single, exclusive interest, a single thought, a single passion—the revolution.*

Nechaev wrote that the revolutionary "has broken every tie with the civil order," and that he will be an "enemy of this world." Destruction will be his only purpose in life. For the revolutionary, everything that "furthers the victory of the revolution" is good, while anything that hinders or slows down the revolution is bad. Finally, Nechaev said that the revolutionary cannot love or have friends; one cold passion must dominate his life and thinking—revolution. He must be willing to murder and be murdered.

In the late seventies, more and more Russian young people turned to terrorism and to the sort of revolution described in the Nechaev's catechism. Movements developed that combined the ideas of the frustrated *narodniki* movement with those of total revolution. Particularly important were two organizations of students founded in the mid and late 1870s. These were the groups called "Land and Liberty," and the later "People's Will." Both groups foreshadowed the more disciplined revolutionaries of the Bolshevik party around Lenin, who would later refer to them as the Russian Revolution in its infancy.

The members of "Land and Liberty" and "People's Will" planned to carry out terrorist acts against those who stood in the way of reform and those involved with the police. One of the first such acts occurred on January 24, 1878, when Vera Zasulich, a young woman who had been interested in radical activity for some time, walked into the headquarters of General Trepov, the governor of St. Petersburg and a man responsible for the torture of many student revolutionaries, and shot him at close range with a pistol. Vera Zasulich's courage was to start a new feeling among the rebels and lead to further assassinations and assassination attempts.

The "People's Will," the most radical of the terrorist groups, sentenced Alexander II to death in 1879. Alexander, who had become czar in 1855, had liberated the serfs and was planning other liberal reforms, but was still considered an enemy by the students. They were successful in carrying out their sentence in 1881, when Alexander was killed by a bomb. His successor, Alexander III (1881–94), was authoritarian and tyrannical; he ordered the secret police to double their efforts against the students. Attempts were made on his life also.

Student activism developed rapidly toward the end of the century. In 1894, students attempted to shout down and force from the university a professor with whom they disagreed. During most of the school years during the nineties, 6 percent of Russia's students were dismissed from school for forbidden political activity. In 1899, more than 13,000 students—around 80 percent of the total number of university students in Russia—went on strike. The nationwide strikes began over a demonstration against an unpopular rector at the University of St. Petersburg. Cossacks were called out, and the students were brutally beaten. Strikes followed in 1901, 1902, and 1904, culminating in 1905 with a rebellion of students and workers that shook all of Russia and that has been called the first stage of the great Revolution of 1917.

Student radicalism diminished after 1905, and by the time of the revolution itself, many young people had become moderates or were no longer politically active. But a groundwork for revolution had been laid. It is difficult to imagine the communist victory of 1917–18 without the efforts of the *narodniki* and early terrorists. Some of Russia's most important revolutionaries had been radical students and played a part in the rebellion we have been describing. Lenin had seen his older brother executed for terrorist activity, and he himself was deeply involved as a young man, as were Stalin and Trotsky. The attitudes they developed as students they carried into their later lives.

The similarities between the Russian student movement and the American New Left are striking. Each movement was leftist and grew more radical as time progressed. Each had a movement "to the people" at the center of its development, and each, in turn, failed to convert the people to revolutionary activity. Both movements experienced deep frustration at this failure and moved toward extremism and terrorism.

But the differences between the two movements are likewise striking. They took place in very different countries under very different conditions. Russia had an authoritarian government, ruling an impoverished and often hungry people; America was a modern, industrialized democracy, governing a largely literate, overly well-fed and well-clothed people. Next, Russian students maintained their anger and revolt for several decades, while American radicals seemed to lose interest in just a few years. Finally, the social origins of American new leftists and Russian *narodniki* diverged markedly. Most American radicals, as we have seen, came from the middle and upper-middle class. Russian populists and radical students came from a variety of classes. The common denominator seemed to be university education which brought them into contact with Western ideas and broke their connection with Russian society and culture. In the Russian student movement, the sons of peasants worked alongside the daughters of nobles; priests' sons joined with the children of merchants.

The second student movement that the New Left has frequently been compared with is the Nazi Youth of the 1920s and 1930s in Germany. The Nazi student organization was perhaps the most tragic of generational conflicts. Young men and women in Germany had been greatly disillusioned by German defeat in World War I. Germany had lost some territory and all her colonies; millions of Germans were included in new nations such as Poland and Czechoslovakia. The nation that had considered itself the greatest of Europe had been reduced to humiliating weakness.

The twenties brought inflation and grave economic problems that seemed insoluble, and these were followed by the depression. Under the circumstances, it is not at all surprising to find young men and women disillusioned, or to find that they condemned those over thirty who had been responsible for the German defeat and humiliation.

The German student movement of the twenties and thirties was a movement of the right, rather than the left. The students were inspired by German history, and their idealism was obsessed with German culture and strength. Students wanted to reunite with Germany the territory lost in the war and to reestablish the German army. By 1930, it had become evident that the leftist political parties of the Weimar Republic had few young members and that the sympathies of the young lay elsewhere. As the temporary prosperity of the late twenties disappeared in the depression, the Nazi party membership grew rapidly, and youthful elements prevailed. To the casual observer in Germany the Nazi party was the party of the future simply because it held the largest number of young people.

The Nazis made a successful appeal to the young people of Germany. An official party slogan ran "Nazism Is the Organized Will of Youth." Another popular slogan attacked the corrupt and inefficient older generation: "Step Down, You Old Ones!" In 1929 and 1930 universities throughout Germany found their student governments dominated by Nazi party members.

The young joined the Storm Troopers, the division of Hitler's followers that was used to terrorize the public and to strike fear in the hearts of Jews and left-wingers. Newspapers were established by Nazi student groups at all universities. These newspapers attacked professors who were not sympathetic to the Nazi cause and ridiculed Jewish professors. A chief characteristic of the German student movement was its anti-Semitism, and frequently the Nazi Youths beat up or threatened Jewish students and shopkeepers.

The violence and intolerance of the Nazi Youth was obvious throughout the early thirties, but came to a head in the spring and summer of 1933. The "brown shirt"—the uniform of the Storm Troopers and Nazi Youth—was introduced by the Nazi young people into the university. They wore the uniform daily to classes and turned the classroom into a military affair. Proclamations were read concerning German nationalism and the military; professors were openly slandered and threatened. Classrooms were repeatedly disrupted by catcalls when a professor said something unpopular with the students.

At Berlin, the rector of the university received an ultimatum of twelve points from the Nazi Youth, ordering him to cleanse the university of its non-German elements. One of the points specified that Jewish professors be required to publish in Hebrew, even though the vast majority of German Jews had spoken German from childhood. The students challenged the rector and told him:

> We honor the few teachers who draw on and teach in the spirit in which we act and live—the spirit of the Storm Troopers. Only these professors have the right to criticize, because they have our confidence.

The attack by the students upon the professors was so complete that many teachers left in despair, or were forced to resign by the universities. The activity of the students reached its climax on May 10, 1933, when they publicly burned the books of fifteen authors in the square opposite the university and beside the Berlin Opera. Those writers whose books the students burned were Jews, Socialists, or others who had attacked the racism, violence, and cruelty of the Nazis.

The students thus greatly helped Adolf Hitler's rise to power and the establishment of the Third Reich. But the students were to be quickly disillusioned, for Hitler moved immediately to bring the universities under his complete control. Traditional student organizations were banned, and the only campus groups remaining were the young Storm Troopers in their brown shirts. Academic freedom no longer existed, and the students found themselves part of an authoritarian society—and that the original purity and sacredness of their cause had been betrayed. By 1943, a whole new generational rebellion had begun, as young radicals, particularly in Munich, began to oppose Hitler and his policies. This was the so-called White Rose Movement, which led to the martyrdom of two of its leaders, Hans and Sophie Scholl. Only the unmitigated brutality of the Nazis prevented this new rebellion from catching on and expanding. It would be the 1960s before the White Rose Movement would find its spiritual descendents and a new German student movement would actively take up leftist causes.

The point of comparison between the Nazi Youth and the New Left has been that both movements were highly self-righteous and intolerant of differing views. Both movements demanded that certain courses be taught and others omitted; both Nazi Youth and the New Left attacked professors they disagreed with and refused to allow them to speak. New leftists were often as rigid as the most intolerant Nazi. Columbia students destroyed the research files of professors they suspected of being pro-Vietnam War or antistudent. Students at other American campuses upset card catalogues in large libraries, totally disrupting the flow of university work. To many older people who recalled the events of Nazi Germany, it seemed as though history were repeating itself through the New Left.

To a large extent they were right. The victim cannot tell the difference between violence exercised by the left and violence exercised by the right. The professor whose life's work is destroyed does not excuse it because those who destroyed it claim to be acting according to a higher morality. The extremists of the New Left were blind to these distinctions and thought that violence used by them was justified because their cause was right and just. But Nazi Youth were likewise persuaded that their violence was right and good.

But the New Left was not entirely a victim of this sort of self-righteous thinking. Much that the New Left accomplished was necessary and good, and in no way connected with violence or force. In final analysis, we must condemn those segments of the New Left that gave way to Nazi-like doctrines, but recognize that the movement as a whole bore little resemblance to the German Youth of the thirties.

# 7 SOME CONCLUSIONS ABOUT THE NEW LEFT

We are now able to draw two sets of conclusions about youthful revolutionary activity. First, we can establish a "model" or pattern that all such revolutions follow and describe characteristics common to all youthful radicals. Second, we can draw conclusions from the course and fate of the New Left and make a conjecture about its future.

The earliest stage in the revolutionary activity of the young begins when students and other people of student age get together in small groups to discuss social problems and elaborate possible solutions. The key phrase of this period might be "What is to be done?" The small groups go on a quest for issues and answers. Young men and women on American campuses were aware of inequality and poverty, talked of injustice, and longed for some way to commit themselves toward improvement of society. Likewise, there were student committees at the Sorbonne, small radical groups at Berlin, and the secret societies of Russian students who prepared the way for action by their discussion and articulation of the problems of their countries.

This early phase is the search for an issue that will be a focus for activity, for the common denominator of all student movements is the urge to act. Once the young have found an issue—civil rights, Vietnam, czarist authoritarianism, German humiliation—then they can act, and act they do. Demonstrations and strikes are usually the first signs of activity. In the beginning, only a dedicated few protest, but their action is seen by many who feel sympathetic and who likewise feel the youthful need to act and change the world. At this time, the youth movement rapidly spreads and enlarges. There is a great amount of generational rebellion present, a feeling among the young that they are attacking their parents. If the parents have failed in some area—have lost a war, have refused to grant blacks equal rights, or have fallen down in whatever issue the youth have decided to act upon—then the generational conflict is severe, and the young "trust no one over thirty."

By this time also in student movements there has developed a strong sense of moral superiority over the rest of society. Not only are the young revolting against their parents, but also they are fighting for a vision that they believe is superior to anything that has gone before. This self-righteousness leads them to believe that their cause is sacred and that they are entrusted with a "special knowledge" and "special virtue" that will allow them, and only them, to improve the social order.

Thus the next stage of activity must be a "to the people" movement. Young Russians wanted to enlighten the peasants. Young Germans wanted to propagandize the Nazi party and turn all true Germans to its cause. The New Left in Japan, France, and Germany, as well as the United States, wanted to go to "the people" and turn them into revolutionaries. In each of these cases, the young revolutionaries had some special information that they had to give the unenlightened public; they had that special knowledge that would save the world.

The generational conflict continues in this "to the people" movement, for the young revolutionaries inevitably define the people as those groups in society most feared and misunderstood by their parents. Thus white middle-class youth in America identified with the black, the French with the Algerian, the modern German with the Jew; the young Russians chose the serf. The young Nazis may appear an exception to this rule, for they did not identify with the poor or "down and out," except to praise, at times, the "racial purity" of the German peasant. Yet the Nazi Youth identified too with those things most feared by some of their parents —with militarism and German nationalism; the German youth embraced those causes that their parents had been too timid to revive.

We have seen how in the cases of the Russian student movement and the New Left, the failure of the "to the people" effort led to frustration and then to terrorism. When the people refused to listen to the special information brought to them by the students, the students were disillusioned and unhappy. But they continued to believe in the sacredness of their cause. It is at this point that the Nazi Youth movement most closely parallels the course of revolutionary youth movements, for the Nazi Youth were above all a group convinced of the sacredness and purity of their cause. Later, however, the young Nazis diverged widely from the standard history of youthful radicalism by becoming an institutionalized arm of the German State and carrying out its policies without question.

In the next stage, terrorist groups spring up. Students lose faith in the political process, and decide the only thing to do is destroy it. SNCC and SDS both grew increasingly radical in the sixties, ending with the Black Panthers and the Weathermen. In Russia, the "People's Will" developed along similar lines. The terrorists bomb and assassinate, and often bring the wrath of the majority down on themselves.

It is with the growth of terrorist organizations that the pattern or "model" of student movements begins to fall apart. In Russia, student activity was maintained over several decades, with periods of partial decline followed by increased activity until after 1905, when a final decline seemed in progress. The New Left, however, except for present-day Germany, seems to have died after only a few years, without realizing its fondest aims and goals. It seems to have had none of the staying power and persistence of the Russian student movement, and little of the vitality and success of the Third World revolutions it so admired. It is now time to ask why the New Left, after running a familiar course with other revolutionary movements of the past, failed to maintain the enthusiasm and devotion of its followers.

The first and most obvious reason for the decline of the New Left is that many of the causes it fought for did not fail at all—they were achieved. Civil rights legislation is part of American law now; the American participation in Vietnam has officially ended. Some universities have restructured themselves to permit a greater student voice in the problems of the school. None of these changes have met the rigorous standards of purity that the New Left demanded, but nevertheless the problems—racism, militarism, and authoritarianism—have seemingly been attacked. The New Left has lost its own causes through partial achievement of its goals.

Next, an equally obvious answer to the decline of the New Left is the unreal nature of student organizations. Students are present at a university for four years, and during those four years they may be active in politics and revolution, but, then they leave, get a job, raise a family, go to graduate school elsewhere; in other words, they pass into a new lifestyle which rarely gives them a chance to be as active in politics as they had been earlier. Jobs and families give them new problems. The freshmen who entered the Sorbonne, Columbia, or Berlin in 1966, left those universities, if they remained to get their degrees, by 1970. By 1971, therefore, a new student body with new interests had come into the universities so bothered by revolution in the sixties. It is impossible to maintain a permanent student radical feeling because there is no permanence to student life. The Russian revolutionaries had maintained their vigor only because Russia was in great need of reform, and because she had a society that refused to accept new ideas. The New Left has been demolished by governments more willing to change and alter, more willing to face problems.

A third explanation for the decline of student activism is psychological. The students in France, Germany, Japan, and America had expressed rebellion against the older generation, and their need to revolt had been satisfied. This satisfaction brought an end to their radical activity. By rebelling, young men and women of the New Left had shown their parents that they were independent and strong; once their point was proved, there was no need for further revolution. Aristotle had noted the same need among the youth of Ancient Greece. He wrote that youthful energy had to find some course of activity, and that this was often in political rebellion against the parents. This rebellion, whether successful or not, would run its course, disappear, and the young would assume their place among the older generation.

There were several roles of generational rebellion that the New Left played. The young, affluent, and privileged young men and women had to find meaning through work with the poor and powerless. They had to attack that strongest of all father figures, the United States. By going among the black, the people of the Third World, and by waging war on the United States, young New Left members the world over proved their manhood and destroyed their parents. When they had done this, they no longer needed the revolutionary roles they had chosen for themselves.

Finally, there were specific problems within the New Left itself that led to its weakness and near disappearance. Much that the New Left demanded was unreal, aimless, and uncertain. Too many members of the New Left refused to compromise with society or the system, and ended up isolated from the power and influence they sought. Politics everywhere and at all times has been the art of graceful compromise; no party, whether conservative, liberal, or radical, has ever achieved its entire program. Many new leftists refused to recognize this very real fact of life. They were too naive and too idealistic, too young and too unreal for this world. They lacked the energy for actual political work, which must be done over long periods of time, and which takes years and years of organization, commitment, and acceptance of frustation and failure. No change ever happens overnight, and this is what the New Left seemed to be seeking. They did not have the dedication and patience of a Mao Tse-tung or a Castro.

Next, the New Left condemned itself by the unclear picture it had of history and of the purpose of rebellion. Often the New Left was at odds with its own principles. The New Left admired Gandhi-like nonviolence and civil disobedience, but likewise came to admire the force and power of guerrilla fighters. It praised democracy and freedom, but utilized manipulation and coercion. The New Left seldom asked itself if the means it employed actually fitted the goals it sought.

The ideas of "participatory democracy" and peaceful change that had been at the heart of the early New Left were abandoned for the romantic appeal of violence and terrorism. The movement that had demanded that government listen to the common man, now refused to listen to anyone. The movement that had fought for votes for blacks in the South, now refused the vote to the South Vietnamese and gave it only to the Vietcong. The movement that had confronted the violence of the police and of society with nonviolence and love, now bombed and killed and called policemen "pigs." This change cannot be called a necessary alteration of method to fit the changing world situation; it cannot be justified entirely by pointing to the frustration and failure of the early movement. No, it seems clear, the New Left forsook its early goals and principles, and in so doing weakened itself and lost the possible sympathy of the majority of people.

This last criticism was particularly true of the New Left in America. In Europe and Japan, where the New Left had been more violent from the very beginning, it does not apply. But a similar criticism does. The violence the young radicals used in these countries was often unnecessary and gratuitous, and done merely for flamboyance or dramatic effect. Japanese students violently attacked police; French students desecrated national shrines. These efforts were self-serving and did nothing to further the revolution; rather, they alienated support and insured the isolation of the young from the rest of society. In whatever country the New Left found itself, it seemed bent on destroying the effectiveness of its own movement.

We have condemned the New Left for many of its shortcomings, but before we ourselves can be accused of self-righteousness and intolerance, we must point to those significant and lasting accomplishments of the New Left. Chapter Five described the continuing success and growth of the German New Left and the demise of New Left effectiveness in France and Japan. In America, young radicals found that many of the ideas and much of the work of the movement came into the mainstream of American politics. The early New Left helped bring about the civil rights legislation, which has gone a long way toward making America a decent place for minority groups. Likewise, the antiwar movement gained success in large part due to the efforts of the young radicals. These are no mean accomplishments, and the New Left can claim responsibility for them.

The ecology and consumer movements were also fed and nourished by the New Left. Young people found that their idealism was challenged by the destruction of the environment, of air, water, and land by pollution. Likewise, Ralph Nader and his investigations into the practices of big business have been influenced by New Left concern for the common man and his rights. In recent years, Nader has turned his attention to government and hopes to improve the quality of American democracy, one of the initial goals of the New Left.

The presidential campaigns of Eugene McCarthy in 1968 and George McGovern in 1972 were spurred on and encouraged by much of the New Left, even though extremists of the movement rejected all compromise with established political parties. Neither McCarthy nor McGovern were successful in their campaigns, but they helped bring the new radicalism before the public. Those who despair of the fate of the New Left would do well to remember that the ideas of the few today are often the ideas of the majority tomorrow.

What the final fate of the New Left is, however, depends upon several factors. Will the governments of the affluent Western countries respond to the social problems raised by bigness, wealth, and power, or will they become, as Daniel Cohn-Bendit argues they already have, rigid bureaucracies without humanity and sensitivity? Will the industrialized countries continue to evolve, reform, and progress, or will they become tyrannies of the contented, as Marcuse argues they have become? In short, we cannot dismiss the New Left, for the problems it raised are still with us and will arouse the idealism of students for generations to come. All that is needed is that special issue, and that special incident which will bring students out into the streets. America, Japan, and Europe are now comparatively quiet, but new generations are being born and growing to maturity that will find their own means of self-expression and rebellion.

# SELECTED READINGS
## BY CHAPTER

### 1: The Watershed Year
The best book on student activity in 1968 is Stephen Spender's *The Year of the Young Rebels* (New York: Random House, also Vintage*, 1968). Spender is an English poet who was a student revolutionary in the 1930s. The best writing on the movement done by a young person is Don McNeill's *Moving through Here* (New York: Alfred A. Knopf, 1970). Less well written is James S. Kunen's description of the Columbia insurrection, *The Strawberry Statement* (New York: Random House, also Avon*, 1969).

### 2: The Heroes, Idols, Art, and Thought
### of the New Left
Besides the books described and listed in the chapter, the reader might find two others interesting. Paul Goodman's *New Reformation* (New York: Random House, also Vintage*, 1970) compares the New Left with the Protestant Reformation, and the New Left leaders with Luther and Calvin. It is one of Goodman's most interesting books. Jeff Nuttall's *Bomb Culture* (New York: Delacorte, 1969) is a rambling, fascinating account of everything that might make a revolu-

* Paperback edition

tionary of modern man. John Gerassi's *Venceremos! The Speeches and Writings of Ernesto Che Guevara* (New York: Simon & Schuster-Clarion\*, 1969) is the best collection of Guevara's words and deeds.

### 3: The Early New Left in America

On the Beatniks, read Bruce Cook's *The Beat Generation* (New York: Charles Scribner's Sons\*, 1971). Jack Newfield's *A Prophetic Minority* (New York: New American Library-Signet\*, 1966) is the best short work on early SNCC and SDS. See also these important works: Anthony Lewis, *Portrait of a Decade: The Second American Revolution* (New York: Random House, 1964) and William McCord, *Mississippi: The Long Hot Summer* (New York: Norton, 1965). Stokely Carmichael's position is summed up in the book he wrote with Charles Hamilton, *Black Power: The Politics of Liberation in America* (New York: Random House-Vintage\*, 1965). For the Free Speech Movement see Michael Miller and Susan Gilmore (eds.) *Revolution at Berkeley* (New York: Dial Press, 1965). For the point of view of a conservative who thought Berkeley had been ruined by its political activity and by its continued involvement with radicalism through 1968 and 1969, see John Coyne's *The Kumquat Statement* (New York: Cowles, 1970). The psychiatrist Kenneth Kenisten, mentioned on p. 44, has written *Young Radicals: Notes on Committed Youth* (New York: Harcourt Brace Jovanovich\*, 1968). The author of the work on generational conflict is Lewis S. Feuer: *The Conflict of Generations* (New York: Basic Books, 1969). Feuer's book is a long thorough study.

### 4: The Vietnam Protest, from Teach-in to Terrorism

A good general work on the New Left is Massimo Teodori (ed.), *The New Left: A Documentary History* (Indianapolis: Bobbs-Merrill\*, 1969). This book contains the important New Left manifestoes, such as "The Port Huron Statement." Louis Menasche and Ronald Radosh (eds.), in *Teach-Ins USA* (New York: F. A. Praeger, 1967), say everything that needs to be said about teach-ins. Alan Adelson's *SDS* (New York: Charles Scribner's Sons\*, 1972) is sympathetic to radicalism and believes that the revised SDS will continue to play an important role in America. Harold Jacobs (ed.), *Weatherman* (San Francisco: Ramparts Press*, 1970) proves beyond a shadow of a doubt that the Weathermen lived all alone in an unreal world. The reader is reminded to take the book with a grain of salt. Very interesting are *Letters from Attica* (New York: William Morrow*, 1972) by Samuel Melville. Melville remains one of the most extraordinary New Left figures. In the book see especially the "Profile of Samuel Melville" by Jane Alpert, a close friend of Melville's. For Lenin's views on the extreme left, see his "Left-Wing Communism: An Infantile Disorder" in *Selected Works of V. I. Lenin* (Moscow: Foreign Languages Publishing House, 1961), Vol. 3, pp. 371–460. For Mao's views on extremists, see Klaus Mehnert, *Peking and the New Left: At Home and Abroad* (Berkeley: Center for Chinese Studies*, 1969).

## 5: The New Left Abroad

There is little available in English about the student movements in Japan, France, and Germany. Very helpful, however, is Marjorie Hope, *Youth Against the World* (Boston: Little, Brown, 1970). Ms. Hope has traveled and lived in all the countries she describes and knows radical young people well. Also interesting is Patrick Seale and Maureen McConville, *Red Flag / Black Flag: French Revolution 1968* (New York: G. P. Putnam's Sons, 1968).

## 6: Young Revolutionaries of the Past

On the Russian revolutionaries, there is Avrahm Yarmolinsky's *Road to Revolution* (New York: Macmillan-Collier*, 1962), a good introduction to the Russian student movement. Also interesting is *The Unmentionable Nechaev* (London: Allen and Unwin, 1961) by Michael Prawdin. A wealth of information and wisdom is had from reading two novels by the great Russian novelist Ivan Turgenev on the radicals of his country: *Fathers and Sons**, which he wrote in 1862, and *Virgin Soil** (1877). Dostoevsky's *The Possessed** is likewise centered on Russian revolutionaries. (These three novels are available in a number of editions.) On the German youth movement see Edward Hartshorne, *The German Uni-*

*versities and National Socialism* (Cambridge: Harvard University Press, 1937) and Walter Laqueur, *Young Germany* (New York: Basic Books, 1962).

Finally the reader is reminded that one of the best places to find out about the New Left is from magazines. *The New York Review of Books, The New Yorker, Life, Esquire, Look,* and *Time* carried countless articles on the young radicals between 1966 and 1970. Also important are the newspapers and journals of the radicals themselves: *Rolling Stone, Radical America, The Village Voice,* and others.

# INDEX

Abolitionists, the New Left as descendant of, 44.

Academic Freedom, and the New Left, in the U.S.A., 39-43, 46-49; in Japan, 64-66; in France, 67-68, 69-72; in Germany, 72-77; and the Russian Student Movement, 80-81, 86; and the Nazi Youth Movement, 88-90.

Advocacy, doctrine of, 40, 42.

Affluence, *see* Family Background of New Left; Wealth, New Left attack on.

Africa, *see* Fanon, Frantz; Colonialism, New Left attack on; Algerian Revolution; Boumedienne, Houari.

*Agrégation,* 70.

Al Fatah, 11.

Alexander II, Czar, 85.

Alexander III, Czar, 85-86.

Algerian Revolution, 11, 13, 15, 24, 68-69, 71, 93.

America, *see* the United States.

The American Indian, 14.

The American Revolution, 12.

Amite County, Mississippi, 34.

Anarchism, 1, 9, 58, 76, 84.

Anti-Americanism and the New Left, in the U.S.A., 2-3, 13, 14, 20, 21, 25-26, 51-52; in Japan, 7, 65, 67; in France, 27, 71; in Germany, 74-75; *see* Generations, Revolt of; Authoritarianism, New Left attack on.

Anti-Semitism and German New Left, 72-73; and the Nazi Youth, 88-89.

Antiwar Movement, in the U.S.A., 2, 3, 4, 46-57, 92, 94, 96; in Japan, 66, 67; in France, 72; in Germany, 74; in the Netherlands, 77; see Vietnam War and the New Left; War Resisters; the Army and the Anti-war Movement.

Aptheker, Herbert, 50.

Arab revolutionaries and the New Left, see Al Fatah; Palestinian Liberation Movement.

Aristotle, 45, 95.

*Armies of the Night,* 16, 51.

The Army and the Antiwar Movement, 52-53; see Antiwar Movement; War Resisters.

Attica Prison Riot, 57.

Authoritarianism, New Left attack on, in U.S.A., 2, 3, 19-20, 21-22, 25-26, 42-43, 55, 59; in Japan, 64-65, 67; in France, 27, 69-72; in Germany, 72-75; and the Russian Student Movement, 80-87; and the Nazi Youth, 87-89, 93; see Bureaucracy, New Left attack on.

*Autobiography of Malcolm X,* 14.


*Baccalauréat,* 70.

Baez, Joan, 17, 41.

Bakunin, Michael, 84.

Baldwin, James, 55.

Bank of America, bomb attack on, 56.

Battista, Fulgencio, 10, 23.

Beards, as revolutionary symbols, 79.

The Beat Generation, 14, 30-31, 44, 77, 100.

The Beatles, 17.

Beatniks, see The Beat Generation.

Berkeley, University of California at, 11, 17, 33, 36, 38, 39-42, 43, 100; teach-in at, 47; People's Park incident, 59; French attitude toward, 71; compared to Free University, 74.

Berlin, New Left in, 11, 12, 23, 73-76; Nazi Youth in, 88.

Berrigan, Father Daniel, 53.

Berrigan, Father Philip, 53.

"Bigness," New Left attack on, see Authoritarianism, New Left attack on; Bureaucracy, New Left attack on.

Black Liberation Movement, 3, 4, 12, 13, 14, 30-36, 39, 58, 68; *see* Black Panther Party.

Black Panther Party, 12, 18, 55, 58, 93.

Bolshevik Party, 85.

"The bomb" and the New Left, 22, 30, 66, 99-100.

Bond, Julian, 34.

Book-burning, by Nazi Youth, 89.

Boumedienne, Houari, 11.

Breitner, Paul, 76.

"Bringing the War Home," 53-54.

Brown, Edmund (Pat), 41.

Brown, John, 55.

The "Brown Shirts," *see* the Storm Troopers.

Bundy, McGeorge, 49.

Bureaucracy, New Left attack on, in U.S.A., 2-3, 39-42; in France, 27-28, 69-72; *see* Authoritarianism, New Left attack on; University reform and the New Left.

Burma, student role in politics, 79.

Cambodia, invasion of, 51-52, 56.

Camus, Albert, 16.

Capitalism, New Left attack on, *see* Wealth, New Left attack on; the Poor and the New Left.

Capitol, U.S., bomb attack on, 57.

Carmichael, Stokely, 35, 58, 100.

Castro, Fidel, 10, 22, 23, 61, 80, 96.

"Castroism: the Long March in Latin America," 22.

*The Catechism of a Revolutionary,* 84-85.

Catonsville Nine, 53.

Charter of Grenoble, 68.

Chase Manhattan Bank, bomb attack on, 57.

Chavez, Cesar, 57.

Che, *see* Guevara, Ernesto "Che."

Chester, Pennsylvania, SDS Project, 38, 42.

Chicago, *see* Democratic National Convention of 1968; Days of Rage.

The Chicago Seven, 25, 58.

Chicano Movement, 57.

Chigirin Uprising of 1877, 83.

China, pre-Communist, student role in politics, 79.

Chinese Revolution, 11, 61-62, 72; French New Left Attitude Toward, 71-72; *see* Mao Tse-Tung.

*La Chinoise,* 18.

Christianity, and the New Left, 32-33, 53; lack of, in Russian Student Movement, 83; *see* King, Dr. Martin Luther; Berrigan, Father Daniel; Berrigan, Father Philip.

CIA (Central Intelligence Agency), 10.

Civil Disobedience, doctrine of, 33, 96; *see* Violence as used by the New Left; Non-violence, doctrine of.

Civil Rights Movement, 13, 17, 30-35, 43; German New Left participation in, 73.

Cleaver, Eldridge, 12-13, 15, 18.

Cohn-Bendit, Daniel, 26-28, 71, 98.

Cohn-Bendit, Gabrielle, 26-27.

The Cold War and the New Left, 21, 30.

Colonialism, New Left attack on, 24-25; *see* Algerian Revolution; Imperialism, New Left attack on; the Third World, New Left identification with.

Columbia University, 2-4, 5, 6, 11, 23, 35, 55, 59, 71, 89, 94, 99.

Communism, and the New Left, in the U.S.A., 12, 20-21, 29, 30, 36, 40, 44, 47, 48, 49, 50; in Japan, 64, 65; in France, 26-27; in Germany, 73, 74, 75, 76; and the Russian Student Movement, 81, 86.

Congress of Racial Equality, see CORE.

Conservatism and the New Left, 4, 19, 25, 42, 43-44.

Consumer Movement, 22, 97.

CORE (Congress of Racial Equality), 33.

Cox, Archibald, Chairman, Committee Investigating Columbia Insurrection, 4.

Cuban Revolution, 10, 57, 58, 61.

Czech Youth and New Left, 78.


Davis, Angela, 12, 21.

"Days of Rage," 55; *see* The Weatherman.

Debray, Regis, 22-24, 27.

The Decembrists, 81.

De Gaulle, Charles, 6, 7, 69, 72.

Democratic National Convention of 1968, 5, 25.

The Demonstration, as tactic of the New Left, 33, 34, 35, 36,

40-41, 46, 49-51; in Japan, 66-67; in France, 66-67; in Germany, 75-76; as tactic of the Russian Student Movement, 86; see the Pentagon March; San Francisco Peace March of 1967; Washington Civil Rights March of 1963; Washington Peace March of 1969.

Desegregation, see Civil Rights Movement; Supreme Court School Desegregation Act.

Deutscher, Isaac, 47.

*Dissent,* 25.

*Doctorat d'état,* 70.

Dohrn, Bernardine, 55, 60.

Dominican Republic, U.S. invasion of, 74.

The Doors, 18.

The Draft and the New Left, 50, 52, 53.

Draft card burning, 52.

Drugs and the New Left, 15.

Dutschke, Rudi, 7, 73, 76.

Dylan, Bob, 15, 16-17, 55.


Earlham College, 37.

East Germany, 74, 75.

Ecology movement, 19, 59, 97.

Education system, New Left attack on, in U.S.A., 2-5, 19-20, 39-41; in Japan, 64-65, 67; in France, 66-67, 70, 72; in Germany, 73, 76; attack on, in Russian Student Movement, 82; in Nazi Youth Movement, 88-89; see Academic Freedom; University reform.

Eisenhower, Dwight D., President, 29, 65.

Emancipation of American Negro, 31.

Emancipation of Russian serf, 80-81, 85.

Encup (Newark Community Union Project), 38, 42.

Engels, Friedrich, quoted, 61.

England, New Left in, 7, 77.

*Eros and Civilization,* 20.

Examination system, French New Left attack on, 70.


Family Background, of New Left, in U.S.A., 44-45; in Japan, 66; in France, 76; in Germany, 76, 77; of Russian Student Movement, 87.

Fanon, Frantz, 14, 22, 24-25.

Guerrilla warfare and the New Left, *see* Terrorism in the extreme New Left; the Third World, New Left identification with; Debray, Regis.

Guevara, Ernesto "Che," 10-11, 14, 16, 18, 22, 23, 28, 76, 80, 100.

Guthrie, Woody, 17.

Gymnasium, question of, at Columbia University, 2-4, 59.

Hamilton, Alexander, 80.

Hanoi, New Left visit to, 49-50.

Harlem, 2.

Harvard University, 38.

Hayden, Tom, 25-26, 27, 36, 49, 58.

Heroes of New Left, 8-17.

Hippie Movement, ii, 13, 15, 19, 50, 51, 77.

Hitler, Adolf, 75, 88-89.

Ho Chi Minh, 11, 80.

Hoffman, Abbie, 58.

Hoffman, Judge Julius, 59.

Holland, *see* the Netherlands.

"Howl," 30.

Hughes, Richard, 48.

Hunter College, 33.

IDA (Institute for Defense Analysis), 2, 3, 4.

Idols of the New Left, 8-17.

Imperialism, New Left attack on, 3, 10, 11, 65, 67; *see* Colonialism, New Left attack on; Israel and the New Left.

Institute for Defense Analysis, *see* IDA.

International Days of Protest, 49.

International Workers of the World, *see* the Wobblies.

Israel and the New Left, 11, 63, 67.

Italy, the New Left in, 7, 77.

Jackson, George, 12, 13.

Japan, New Left in, 1, 7, 63-67, 92, 96, 97.

Jaspers, Karl, 74.

Jefferson, Thomas, 79.

The Jefferson Airplane, 18.

Jeffersonian ideals of New Left, 36.

McCarthy, Senator Eugene, 5, 97.
McCarthy, Senator Joseph, 30.
McGovern, Senator George, 97.
Madison, James, 79-80.
Mailer, Norman, 15-16, 47, 51.
Manhattan Federal Building, bomb attack on, 57.
Mao Tse-tung, 11, 14, 16, 39, 61-62, 76, 96, 101.
Maoism, among American young people, 49, 50; in the films of Jean-Luc Godard, 18.
The March, as tactic and activity of the New Left, *see,* Demonstration, as tactic of the New Left.
Marcuse, Herbert, 20-22, 98.
Marine Midland Bank, bomb attack on, 57.
Marx, Karl, 12, 14, 42, 61.
Marxism, of the German New Left, 73-74, 75.
The May Days, 26-28, 71-72.
May Second Movement, M-2-M, 49.
Melville, Samuel, 57, 62, 101.
Michigan, University of, 36, 37, 38, 47.
Miike Mine Strike, 66.
Milan, University of, 77.
Militarism, New Left attack on, in the U.S.A., 2-3, 20-22, 39, 46-57; in Japan, 64; in Germany, 74; *see* Antiwar Movement; The Army and the Antiwar Movement; the Draft and the New Left; Authoritarianism, New Left attack on.
Minnesota, University of, 17, 33.
Mississippi Freedom Delegation to the Democratic National Convention of 1964, 34.
Montgomery Bus Boycott, 31.
Moscow, University of, 81.
Mozambique, rebels in, 78.
Music of the New Left, 16-18.

Nader, Ralph, 97.
Nanterre University, 2, 6, 70.
Napoleon, 80.
*Narodniki* Movement, 82-87.
National Conference for New Politics, *see* NCNP.
National Coordinating Committee to End the War, 49.

National Student Association, *see* NSA.

National Union of French Students, *see* UNEF.

Nazi Youth Movement, 75, 80, 87-90, 93, 101-102; *see* Storm Troopers.

Nazism and the German New Left, 73, 74-75.

NCNP (National Conference for New Politics), 54.

Nechaev, Sergei, 84-85, 101.

The Netherlands, the New Left in, 77.

New Haven Black Panther Trial, 58.

*New Left Notes,* 55.

New York Peace March of 1967, 50.

Newark Community Union Project, *see* Encup.

Newark Riots of 1967, 25.

Newton, Hughie, 12.

Nicholas I, Czar, 81.

Nihilism, 82.

Nixon, Richard, 48, 53.

Nonviolence, doctrine of, 17, 33, 96; *see* Christianity and the New Left; SNCC.

North Carolina Agricultural and Technical College, 32.

NSA (National Student Association), 38.


Oberlin University, 37.

*Obsolete Communism: the Left-Wing Alternative,* 26-27.

Odetta, 16.

Ohnesorg, Benno, 76.

The Old Left, in the U.S.A., 29, 36, 42, 44, 49, 50; in Japan, 64, 65; *see* Communism and the New Left; the Social Democratic Party of Germany.

*On the Road,* 31.

*One Dimensional Man,* 20.

*One Plus One,* 18.

Ono, Yoko, 17.


Palestinian Liberation Movement, 63.

Parks, Mrs. Rosa, 31.

Parris, Bob, 34, 35.

Participatory democracy, doctrine of, 26, 37-39, 47, 96.

Peace and Freedom Party, PFP, 54.

The Peace Corps and the New Left, 50.

Peace Movement, *see* Antiwar Movement.

The Pentagon March, 50, 52.

People's Park of Berkeley, 59.

"People's Will," 85, 93.

Peter, Paul and Mary, 18.

Pilgrims, New Left as descendants of, 44.

Plato, 45.

Poland, youth in, 78.

The Police, and the New Left, at Columbia University, 4; at the Democratic National Convention, 5; in the French May Days, 6; in the Civil Rights Movement, 32, 33; at Berkeley, 40-41, 59; and violent antiwar activists, 55-56.

Political Movement, definition of a, 9.

*The Politics of Ecstasy,* 15.

The Poor, and the New Left, 25-26, 31-39; and the Russian Student Movement, 80-84; *see* Wealth, New Left attack on; the Third World, New Left identification with.

Popular opinion of the New Left, 4-5, 42, 56, 59.

Port Huron Convention of the SDS, 37.

Port Huron Statement, 37-38, 100.

Posters of the New Left, 9, 11, 12, 16.

Princip, Gavrilo, 80.

Progressive Labor Party, PL, 50, 54, 55.

Prohibitionists, the New Left as descendants of, 44.

The Provos, 77.

Puritanism in the New Left, in the U.S.A., 44, 60; in Japan, 66; in youth movements in general, 92-93.

Racism, New Left attack on, in U.S.A., 2, 3, 12, 13, 31-36, 39, 42; in France, 68-69; in Germany, 73; of Nazi Youth, 88-89.

RCA Building, bomb attack on, 57.

Reagan, Ronald, 59.

*Rebellion in Newark,* 25.

The Red Guards, 62.

Religion and the New Left, ii, 15, 32-33, 53; *see* Christianity and the New Left.

*Revolution in the Revolution?,* 22-23.

Robespierre, Maximilien, 80.

The Rolling Stones, 17-18.

Romanticism, as a Youth Movement, i-ii.

Rome, University of, 77.

Rostow, Walt, 49.

ROTC, Reserve Officers' Training Corps, New Left attack on, 39, 52, 56.

Rubin, Jerry, 58.

Rudd, Mark, 3, 55, 60.

Rusk, Dean, 48.

Russian Orthodox Church, 82.

Russian Revolution, 12, 54, 61, 86.

Russian Revolution of 1905, 86.

Russian Student Movement, 80-87, 92, 93, 94, 101.

Rutgers University, 33, 48.


St. Just, L. A., 80.

St. Petersburg, University of, 81, 86.

San Francisco Peace March of 1967, 50.

Sartre, Jean-Paul, 16, 72.

Savio, Mario, 40, 41.

Scholl, Hans, 89.

Scholl, Sophie, 89.

SCLC (Southern Christian Leadership Conference), 33.

SDS (German Socialist Student Union), 72-75.

SDS (Students for a Democratic Society), 3, 15, 36-39, 46, 49, 50, 54, 55, 58, 72, 93, 100, 101.

Seale, Bobby, 58.

Selective Service System, see the Draft and the New Left.

Self-righteousness of the New Left, in the U.S.A., 19, 43, 44, 52, 60, 62; in Japan, 66, 67; in France, 66-67, 71-72; of the Nazi Youth, 88-89; of youth movements in general, 92.

The Selma Civil Rights March, 35.

The Shah of Iran, 75-76.

The Silent Generation, 29.

The Sit-in, 32, 33.

SNCC (Student Nonviolent Coordinating Committee), 33, 34, 37, 39, 40, 55, 93, 100.

SNCC Manifesto, 35-36.

Social Democratic Party of Germany, 72-73.

The "Society of Communists," 81.

*Soledad Brother,* 12, 13-14.

Soledad Prison Riot, 14.

The Sorbonne, University of Paris, 6, 10, 23, 70-72, 79, 91, 94.

*Soul on Ice,* 12-13.

The South and the New Left, 13, 30-36; *see* Civil Rights Movement; the Selma Civil Rights March.

Southern Christian Leadership Conference, *see* SCLC.

Spock, Dr. Benjamin, 51.

Spontaneity, in character of New Left, in U.S.A., 42; in Japan, 65, 66; in Germany, 73; *see* Fanon, Frantz.

Springer, Axel, 76.

Stalin, Joseph, 29, 47, 86.

Stone, I. F., 47.

Storm Troopers, 88-89; *see* Nazi Youth Movement.

Student Nonviolent Coordinating Committee, *see* SNCC.

*Studenten Vakbeweging,* 77.

The "Summer Project" of 1964, 34.

The Supreme Court School Desegregation Act, 30-31.

Swarthmore College, 37, 38.

Teach-ins, 46-49, 52, 100.

Technology, New Left analysis of, 19-20, 21-22, 28.

Tel Aviv Airport massacre, 63, 67; *see* Japan, New Left in.

Terrorism, in the films of Godard, 18; in the thought of Fanon, 24-25; in the extreme New Left of the U.S.A., 51-52, 55-57, 59-60; of Japan, 63, 67; of France, 72; of Germany, 76; of Italy, 77; in the Russian Student Movement, 83-86; in the Nazi Youth Movement, 88; as a characteristic of youth movements in general, 93; *see* the Third World, New Left identification with; Algerian Revolution; Debray, Regis.

The Third World, New Left identification with, 11, 24-25, 48, 57, 63, 69, 73, 78, 94, 95.

Thought of the New Left, 19-21.

Tolerance and the New Left, *see* Academic Freedom; University reform; Free Speech Movement; Self-Righteousness of the New Left.

Trepov, General, 85.

*Trial,* 25.

Trotsky, Leon, 12, 47, 86.
Trotskyites, 65.
The Tupamaros Guerrillas, 11.
Turgenev, Ivan, 82, 101.
Turin, University of, 77.
Turkey, rebels in, 78.

UNEF (National Union of French Students), 67-71.
United Fruit Company, bomb attack on, 57.
United States, New Left in, 1-5, 29-62, 91, 92, 93, 94, 95, 96, 97.
University reform, as goal of the New Left in the U.S.A., 2-5, 32, 39-42; in Japan, 64-67; in France, 66, 68-71, 72; in Germany, 73, 76; Russian Student Movement's efforts to obtain, 81, 86; Nazi Student Movement's efforts to obtain, 88-89.
Uruguay, rebels in, 78.

Veterans Against the War, 50.
The Vietnam War and the New Left, in the U.S.A., 2, 5, 23, 34, 46-57, 92, 94, 96; in Japan, 67; in France, 71; in Germany, 74, 76; in the Netherlands, 77.
Violence, as used by the New Left, in the U.S.A., 2-5, 51, 53-58, 59, 61, 96; in Japan, 63, 66-67; in France, 66, 72; in Germany, 67, 76; in Italy, 67, 77; uselessness of violence as tactic, 96-97; as used against the New Left, *see,* the Police and the New Left; Kent State University.
Voter Registration, 33, 39.

War Resisters, in Canada, 51, 52; in Sweden, 53; *see* the Army and the Anti-war Movement; the Draft and the New Left.
Waseda University, 67.
Washington Civil Rights March of 1963, 34.
Washington Peace March of 1969, 51.
Wealth, New Left Attack on, 14, 19-20, 21-22, 25-26, 30-31; during May Days in France, 6-7; *see* the Third World, New Left identification with.
The Weatherman, 15, 23-24, 55-57, 60-62, 93, 101.
*Weekend,* 18.

# ABOUT
# THE AUTHOR

Stephen Goode is a member of the history faculty of Rutgers University, specializing in European social and intellectual history. He holds degrees from Davidson College, the University of Virginia, and Rutgers and has studied at Debrecen University in Hungary and the University of Vienna. Mr. Goode is a resident of Highland Park, New Jersey.